POWER SALES
PRESENTATIONS

Also by Stephan Shiffman

Closing Techniques (That Really Work!)
Cold Calling Techniques (That Really Work!)
The Consultant's Handbook
*The 25 Sales Habits of Highly Successful Salespeople,
2nd Edition*
*The 25 Most Common Sales Mistakes
(and How to Avoid Them), 2nd Edition*
Power Sales Presentations
Stephan Schiffman's Telemarketing

POWER SALES PRESENTATIONS

Complete Sales Dialogues
for Each Critical Step of
the Sales Cycle

Stephan Schiffman

BOB ADAMS, INC.
PUBLISHERS
Holbrook, Massachusetts

Published by Adams Media Corporation
260 Center Street, Holbrook, MA 02343

ISBN: 1-55850-252-1

Printed in the Canada.

J   I   H   G   F   E   D

This publication is designed to provide accurate and authoritative
information with regard to the subject matter covered. It is sold with
the understanding that the publisher is not engaged in rendering legal,
accounting, or other professional advice. If legal advice or other
expert assistance is required, the services of a competent professional
person should be sought.
— From a *Declaration of Principles* jointly adopted by
a Committee of the American Bar Association and a
Committee of Publishers and Associations

Cover design: Marshall Henrichs.

This book is available at quantity discounts for bulk purchases.
For information, call 1-800-872-5627 (in Massachusetts, 617-767-8100).

Visit our home page at http://www.adamsmedia.com

Acknowledgments

I'd like to thank the following people for their assistance with this book:

Brandon Toropov for his help in developing the material and seeing it through to the finished product; Marcela Deauna for her support and patience with the preparation of the manuscript; Michele Reisner for her editorial work and assistance in organizing the manuscript; Steve Bookbinder for providing the input from the "front lines"; Kate Layzer for her invaluable copyediting aid; and finally, the thousands of salespeople we meet each year who fully appreciate the frustrations, challenges, and rewards of selling.

This book is dedicated, with love, to
WLS and MFS.

Contents

Introduction

Congratulations! By buying this book, you have put yourself ahead of 90 percent of all salespeople. The vast majority of people in our field do not take the time to invest in
their own professional development, and that's a big mistake. You've already joined that elite 10 percent who know
how essential it is to monitor one's personal sales progress.
Now this book is going to reward you for your motivation.

The techniques covered here will put you ahead of
the pack at every phase of the sales process, from your initial interaction with a potential customer to closing a sale.
We will not be talking about dry theories and scholarly
analyses in *Power Sales Presentations*. These techniques
have been throughly tested and refined by real salespeople—myself included.

You probably don't need anyone to tell you that sales
can sometimes be a challenging way to make a living. Still,
I do think it's important to let you know here that real-
world advice for real-world problems is the order of the day
in my programs. Put more simply, *I know what you're up
against.* I sell every day; my service is sales training programs. And that means two things. First, I am no stranger
to the daily rejection, repetition, and morale deflation that
is every salesperson's lot. And second, over the years, I've
worked with a whole lot of salespeople. What I've learned
from working with them can make you money.

In the course of working with and listening to thousands upon thousands of sales representatives, I have learned some important things about how to sell effectively. This book will cover, among many other topics:

- Prospect management: A unique system that drives the sales process and helps you evaluate where you are in the sales cycle.

- How to handle objections: A step-by-step approach to the sales process that brings you and your prospect to a common goal.

- Questions: What are the three most important questions you can ask the prospect? What is the best way to frame them?

- Closing: How to work *with* the prospect so that you know exactly when to initiate the final stage of the sale—and get a "yes."

That last point is of particular interest to virtually all salespeople. Although the close is a *result*, not a stage you can impose upon the prospect, it *is* something you can guide to your advantage. Many salespeople are taught that there's a mystique to closing, and, therefore, to selling in general. "Either you have it or you don't," goes the thinking. Don't believe it.

In actual fact, selling is a logical, step-by-step progression. It doesn't have to be difficult. It doesn't have to be complicated. By the time you finish this book, you'll know how to close a sale simply by saying,

---

Mr. Prospect, I feel that everything I've discussed today really makes a lot of sense for your organization. What do you think? Can we go ahead?

It really can be that easy.

✦　　✦　　✦

Let me ask you something. How many in-person sales calls did you make last year? I made 353.

If you weren't quite sure of the figure, you can rest assured you're not alone. Most salespeople are unable to give even a vague estimate of the number.

It's funny, isn't it? We know what mileage our car gets, what our monthly phone bill is, how much is in our bank account—and yet the chances are we *don't* know how many in-person sales calls we made, or—and this is the important part—*how successful we were.*

I'm going to help you change that. I'm also going to help you use your time more effectively, sell more effectively, make more money, and best of all, enjoy what you're doing. Believe me, selling really can be great fun for you. It is for me!

✦　　✦　　✦

As I mentioned, I speak with thousands of salespeople every year; it's in listening to them that I have been able to formulate and refine the principles embodied in this book.

In the same way, I want to listen to you. If you have any comments on this book, positive or negative, I'd like to hear them. What worked best for you? Where were there problems? What would you like to see addressed in subsequent titles?

This book is your book. To the extent that it offers solutions to problems you face regularly, it's successful. To the extend that it doesn't, I'd like to know about how my systems can serve as a better tool for you in your sales work.

Here's my address:

Stephan Schiffman
c/o Bob Adams, Inc./ Publishers
260 Center St.
Holbrook, MA 02343

✦   ✦   ✦

There are a lot of books on sales. It comes as no surprise, then, that there are a lot of bad books on sales.

It's true. Quite a few unfortunate misconceptions surround the profession of selling. You probably run into one or two of them every day.

For my part, I love sales work. It's what I do best. No matter what people who don't do it for a living may think, it's an honorable calling, one I'm very proud to call mine. Accordingly, it makes me mad when people pass around a lot of nonsense, either on a bookshelf or at a sales meeting, that gets in the way of salespeople performing up to their potential.

Just to put your mind at ease, I've assembled here a (non-exhaustive) list of foolish things people say or write about selling for a living—things you won't encounter here.

"Salespeople are born, not made."

"The best salespeople have their eye on closing the sale from the minute they walk in the door."

"When you can't dazzle 'em with brillance, baffle 'em with . . . "

"All you have to do is learn how to sell. The appointments, the prospecting, all that stuff will take care of itself."

"Probe the prospect, if only to keep him talking. It doesn't matter about what."

"Always try to close on the first visit."

"Never try to close on the first visit."

"Good salespeople don't have to make cold calls."

"Sales always is and always will be high-pressure, high-conflict work. If you can't stand the heat, get out of the kitchen."

"Your leads make all the difference—once you have a top-notch list, you don't have to qualify."

"Don't worry about your statistics; that's the sales manager's job."

"The nice thing about sales—particularly telephone sales—is that you have a lot more leeway about your personal appearance around the office. If you don't want to dress to the nines every morning, it really doesn't make any difference."

"All the listening in the world can't change the fact that you are trying to win over the prospect. If you have to choose between listening and going for the jugular, go for the jugular."

There. Now that we've gotten that nastiness out of the way, it's time to talk about you and your work as a salesperson. Where do we start?

On a baseball diamond in Cleveland, Ohio, about seventy years ago. Where else?

Chapter One

The Triple Play

My nominee for best undiscovered salesperson of 1920

On October 10, 1920, something happened in World Series play that had never happened before—and has never happened since. It happened to a fellow named Bill Wambsgnass, who was, on that day, playing second base for the Cleveland Indians in the fifth game of the 1920 Series against the Brooklyn Dodgers.

In a tight game, with men on first and second and nobody out, the Dodgers' batter, Clarence Mitchell, hit a sharp line drive to the left side of the infield. Wambsgnass speared it—one out. Then, in a split second, he realized that the runner on second had taken a lead too far from the bag. There Wambsgnass was on second, all alone! He tagged the bag with his left foot—two outs.

That's when the routine play became something truly incredible. The runner on first, Otto Miller, had misjudged the ball and taken off for second a bit too eagerly. Wambsgnass saw the terrified Miller caught halfway between the bases, charged over, and applied the tag—three outs.

Bill Wambsgnass had completed the first unassisted triple play in World Series history. No one has done it in Series play since.

Why am I talking about baseball in a book that's supposed to tell you about sales? Simple. I think Bill

Wambsgnass had the makings of a great salesperson, and I'll tell you why.

Nobody can "strategize" a triple play. The manager can't signal for one from the bench. It's a long shot. The very best baseman in the league (which, by the way, Wambsgnass was not) couldn't have anticipated that play intellectually. Such an event can only be executed by instinct, when a certain set of circumstances arises in front of someone who can react quickly and effectively to sudden opportunity.

By the same token, there is no "average sale." As any experienced salesperson will tell you, each and every sale is a long shot . . . typically, as we'll learn, a 20-to-1 long shot. Not, perhaps, as rare as an unassisted triple play, but just as dependent on a solid grounding in the fundamentals of your "game."

Bill Wambsgnass was prepared. The situation developed; he responded appropriately and wrote himself into the history books. He couldn't have done that without the constant drilling and practice that is an integral part of the game of baseball at the major-league level. He couldn't have done it if he'd come to the ballpark that day without the right tools, or without warming up, or having skipped his last two or three meals.

In the same way, you, as a salesperson, must be prepared. You have to work at the fundamentals, over and over again, until they're second nature. That's the purpose of this book; to familiarize you with the soundest techniques you can use to move your sales through identifiable stages. And, contrary to what you may believe, every sale does have distinct stages—just like Wambsgnass's triple play!

There are scripts . . . and there are scripts

Many salespeople recoil in horror at the very notion of a script, even the open-ended kind I'm suggesting in this book. "I'll sound awful! I'll sound canned! It'll be so fake, no one will take me seriously! I can't work from a script!" I usually answer those kinds of objections with a story from my days as a beginning driver.

It didn't matter who was in the car with me or what I would do ahead of time— I used to be terrified of driving. I mean, absolutely petrified. After all, there was so much to remember. Shift. Turn signal. Turn wheel. Shift. Change lane. Check mirror. On and On. Was I really supposed to memorize all this? How did people ever know what to do next? What on earth was going to happen out there?

Once, I was so concerned about all the things I was supposed to be doing while I was in the driver's seat that I actually drove with the right rear passenger door open—for a quarter of a mile! As you might expect, I got some pretty strange looks out on the street.

Now, I think everybody can identify with those first few weeks of driving out on the highway. Those kinds of butterflies are natural, after all. Here's the big question, though. If everyone has to deal with that stage of being unable to remember all the things you have to do while you're driving, how can anybody get anywhere without smashing into something?

Of course, the answer is that, after a while, it becomes instinctive. There are still just as many things for you to do in the car today as there were when you first buckled up to get ready for your driving test. The difference is, by this point, you've drilled the fundamentals so thoroughly that you don't even have to think about them. Nevertheless, you are still following a set pattern—one you can adjust for unexpected developments.

That's exactly the role your script will play for you. It will allow you to follow a set pattern—but adjust quickly for sudden changes.

You don't have to sound canned or fake or machine-like. As a matter of fact, that's all completely opposite to what a script is supposed to do for you. Honest!

Think about it. What's your favorite movie? Stop and think about that film for a second. Now, ask yourself; the last time you were watching it, did you say to yourself, "Gee, this sure is forced, canned, and unnatural."?

Chances are, you didn't. But every word, every movement, every gesture was almost certainly planned out in meticulous detail ahead of time by the filmmakers! Moviemakers virtually always require much greater attention to detail and control over their work than you'll ever have to worry about in yours—yet the final product rings true. The whole point of a script is to be fluid, genuine, real. That's what Meryl Streep expects from her scripts. There's no reason for you to accept anything less.

"Dress Rehearsals"

The main idea that underlies the work we'll be doing in this book is that your sales environment is much more familiar to you than it is to anyone else. It's certainly more familiar to you than it is to the potential customer!

While the setting in which the customer uses your product or service is unique, you—and only you—are in a position to apply the lessons learned from common problems and opportunities that have arisen with previous customers. There will almost certainly be points of contact between the experiences you've shared with your existing customer base and the experiences of the people you want to turn into customers. Once you realize that, you begin to learn that your environment provides you with the opportunity to prepare for certain predictable events—and to anticipate your best reactions to those events.

Now, when it comes right down to it, wouldn't you rather develop your strategies, make your mistakes, and get your sudden inspirations before you walk into the client's office? Sure you would. And that's where this book comes in. Consider the techniques and scenarios in this book, then, to be "dress rehearsals"—risk-free opportunities to prepare for the challenges that will probably arise at some point in any given sale.

And, yes, you read that right. I said "any given sale." I've found, over the years, that all sales, whether of radishes or software or furniture or missile systems or anything else you care to name, can, for the salesperson, be broken down into four distinct stages:

Qualifying
Interviewing
Presentation
Closing

I'd suggest that, after reading this book, you find a partner and work your way through each of the four stages with some role-playing. Some salespeople don't feel this "improvising" approach is for them, but I've found that it really is invaluable in customizing the techniques to your specific situation. Again: if you have to blow it sometime, why not blow it, to the greatest degree possible, in front of a friend (who can't give you a sale anyway) rather than a prospect (who can)?

Once you've taken care of all that, you'll be prepared to turn some triple plays of your own . . . and make Power Sales Presentations.

When I refer to Power Sales Presentations, I'm not just throwing buzzwords at you. I'm talking abut specific, highly effective selling skills, based on the boxed sales dialogues included in this book. These line-by-line exchanges aren't really "scripts" so much as dynamic examples of how the techniques we'll be talking about can be employed in the real world. Each sales dialogue draws on the combined sales experience of the hundreds of thousands of salespeople I've worked with over the years.

The sales dialogues are, first and foremost, keys to your success as a salesperson. They offer specific phrases and sequences of questions you can use in your sales work to generate more sales and put your career on the fast track. They're outlines of the very best ways you can work with a potential customer, identify common goals and more effectively do your job—help the customer.

Helping the customer. It sounds simple, but it's a lot rarer than you think. In fact, to my way of thinking, it's the sales equivalent of turning the unassisted triple play. But here's the payoff: Wambsgnass did it once. You can do it for a living, every day.

How? We'll find out in chapter 2 by taking a look at the tools you'll be using.

SUMMARY
Chapter One: The Triple Play

✔ Constant drilling and practice are an integral part of "major league" sales work.

✔ The fact that you use a script does not mean that you have to sound fake or machine-like.

✔ Your sales environment is much more familiar to you than anyone else, including your potential customer.

✔ The scenarios in this book represent risk-free opportunities for you to prepare for the challenges that will probably arise at some point in any given sale.

✔ All sales can be broken down, for our purposes, into four distinct stages.

Chapter Two

The Tools

This book will supply you with specific suggestions and guidelines on what to say in arranging and conducting a sales appointment.

We'll be looking at this topic in a very hands-on way. If you want to use the scripts I'll supply you with word-for-word, you can do that; if you want to adjust the scripts for your own use, taking into account your own experience with your market and your product, feel free.

Obviously, I'm not an expert in your field. There are any number of approaches you can take that might work like gangbusters in real estate but fail spectacularly when it comes to selling insurance. My basic philosophy is that if you find something that works for you, use it—I'm not going to tell you to change a winning formula. And I mean that. If you find that you can consistently close sales by walking up to your prospect and telling him, "Hey, Mr. Jones, you know what, that tie you're wearing is the ugliest thing I've ever seen in my life," then keep using that line.

But this book, after all, covers what I've learned about sales dialogues over years of work with thousands of prospects and tens of thousands of salespeople. I've developed a system that I've found works consistently, in just about any situation, for the vast majority of sales professionals. So that's what I'm passing along.

Take and use as much of it as you're comfortable with, and as much as makes sense in your sales environment. Before you go wild with innovation, though, let me caution you on a couple of points.

One of the main principles I've developed over the years is that the absolute basics of the game are pretty much the same in any selling situation. When it comes right down to it, it's not that productive to get hung up on the differences between products that various salespeople sell. That's because the fundamental idea behind any product or service is that it *fulfills the need or desire of a given customer*. That goes for software or soft-serve ice cream, for automats or automobiles, for rock videos or rocket launching systems. If it doesn't make a customer happy, it's not worth selling. If it does make a customer happy, it is.

A parallel principle I've used in developing this system is a little more difficult to swallow at first glance, but it really makes just as much sense. That is that it is absolutely impossible to make a sale to IBM.

Or Chrysler. Or Coca-Cola. Or Joe's Taxi.

Surprised? Hear me out. When you walk into the prospect's office, do you shake hands with a logo? Do you make your presentation to a box of stationery? Do you lean out the window and talk about your product's benefit to the granite and glass and steel they used to build corporate headquarters?

No. You're talking to a person. A person in a room who has a problem that you can solve.

Those are the terms in which you must view your work. The fact that John Smith is the vice-president of umpty-ump or the manager of la-de-da is good information for you to have, but it's not the only information you need, and it's probably not the most crucial. Nor is the fact that his company is the most prestigious one in the world, though it's certainly something to bear in mind as you define your approach.

What you must accept, however, is that in order to

close the sale you must *work to identify John Smith's problems*. The most important fact about John Smith, when it comes right down to it, is not that he works for IBM or any of those other companies, but that he is a guy in a room who's agreed to talk to you because you may be able to save him money, make his business or department more efficient, or increase his profits.

That's why my company's definition of selling is: "Asking people what they do, how they do it, when they do it, where they do it, and why they do it, and helping them do it better."

"Asking." That's the key word here. Not "selling," as so many salespeople believe, and as so many misguided sales trainers have led them to believe. Asking is crucial to your success as a salesperson. After all, if you don't ask, how will you know what the customer does, or why they do it this way? And if you don't know what those wants, desires, or needs are, how can you fulfill them?

You have to be able to ask. In chapter 5, we will go into detail about how to frame questions properly in order to get the information you will need to ask the right questions.

You can't close company X. You can close John Smith if you know how to help him do his job better.

#1: The fundamental idea behind the sale of any product or service is that it fulfills the needs or desires of a given customer.

#2: The prospect is not an institution, but a person with a problem you can solve with your product or service.

Now it's time to talk about the specifics.

Familiarizing yourself with your tools

You'll be using a number of tools to improve your performance as a salesperson and get the most out of this book. We're going to list them here, as well as some tips on how to use them most effectively.

Tool number one: Your Product

What's the product (or service) you're putting your name on? It's your livelihood we're talking about, and you must know it inside and out. What makes it different, better, more effective? Specifically, how does it help your customer, compared to using someone else's product? Compared to using nothing at all? Compared to another model? You have to know these things. If you don't, there's no way you can relate the benefits to a potential customer.

Put yourself in your customer's shoes. Try to get to know all the ins and outs of the product; take some time to use it for a day, if that's possible. If that's not possible, do some serious role-playing and do your darndest to be the customer for a day. What do you find out about the product or service? Are you happy with it? Why or why not?

Tool number two: Yourself

You probably already know that your health, fitness, and positive outlook constitute important elements in your overall happiness and well-being. This, of course, includes attention to such things as eating well, exercising regularly, and staying away from drug or alcohol abuse. You may be surprised to learn, however, that the "you" you present to the outside world is also one of your most important sales tools. Your image, if you like.

How will a potential customer perceive you?

If you have some doubts on this score—or, even worse, if you have no idea what the answer to the question is—it's time to look at your image more closely. The reason's quite simple. To the customer, you are the product. If you come across unprofessionally, there's virtually nothing that can repair the damage and win the sale.

It's a fact. How you look will be a determining element in whether or not you are going to get a business. That doesn't mean every salesperson has to look like a professional model, but it does mean that you cannot afford to be lackadaisical about your appearance. To sell something to someone else, you must inspire trust and respect.

You may remember the episode of the television show "L.A. Law" that featured a defense attorney who happened to be a dwarf. This character made a very important point about physical appearances. He pointed out that the turning point in his legal career had been learning to accept the fact that people would always look at him differently because of his size. Once he accepted that, the lawyer went on, he learned to use that fact to his advantage in the courtroom, and not to feel victimized by his own body.

To a certain extent this is true for all of us; it's especially true for those of us who don't happen to be "textbook" attractive in the same way that some movie stars or models are. If you have a large nose, a receding hairline, or some other prominent feature that might be considered a "disadvantage," it's imperative that you accept yourself—that you develop a positive self-image and a sense that you are worth talking to in the first place.

"Disadvantages" are only what you let them be. "Disadvantages" didn't stop Stephen Hawking from becoming a brilliant physicist, and they didn't stop Franklin Roosevelt from being a great president. Nobody's perfect; nobody's you. Start from the beginning. Know how people react to the "equipment" you bring to the appointment, and learn how to use those reactions to your advantage.

I'm five feet seven inches tall. I have black hair. I wear glasses. I'm rather thin. I don't pretend that I'm the spitting image of Clark Gable. I'm Stephan Schiffman. If I'm making a presentation to a group of thirty people, each of whom is six feet four and weighs two hundred and forty pounds, I'm going to adjust my approach. Perhaps, in that setting, even if I customarily stand to deliver my presentation to a group, I'm going to take a seat at one end of the tale—to try to minimize the size differential.

As far as your actual attire is concerned, it's really nothing more than a matter of simple professionalism. A doctor conveys a sense of authority by wearing a clean, white smock, not a bathrobe. A top trial lawyer would never think of walking into a courtroom in a pair of jeans, or with a cigarette dangling from her mouth, or wearing a torn or soiled jacket. The same applies to you.

When you make a sales call, professional attire will tell the person looking at you that you mean business—that you understand what you do for a living and why, and that your main goal is to convey information and knowledge as a result of your meeting. You're not there to hassle, or convince, or make someone buy something against his or her will. You're there to offer your product or service in the most professional manner possible. And you've taken the time to prepare for this appointment because the prospect is the most important person you're going to see during the next hour or so.

Too many salespeople forget this. They forget how important it can be for them to look and act the part of a professional. They think the product will sell itself—and that just isn't so.

Tool number three: Your Personal Contact Network (and how to expand it)

Tell everyone what you do, every chance you get. And do it proudly. I don't care if you've been selling for a week, or a month, or a year, or every day of your life. Always broadcast what you do for a living to anyone and everyone who'll listen. Word of mouth is one of the most cost-effective ways to solicit leads; people you talk to may (and probably do) know someone who needs your service. Talk yourself up.

For some strange reason, many salespeople don't want to do this. They go to a party, they meet people, they talk, and when one of the most common questions in the English language—"What do you do for a living?"—comes up, what does the salesperson say?

Out comes this tiny, barely audible whisper: "I, ah . . . I sell services . . .", or "I'm involved in some marketing-related projects, just now, that is . . . ", or "Me? Oh, I, well, I work in this bank."

Why on earth don't you hear the person shouting, "I sell financial services for XYZ Bank!"

Try it. Take the initiative. Tell people what you do without waiting for them to ask. It's a secret that most successful people swear by. Let the word get out about how well you do your job and how great your product is. Chances are, you'll hear from someone inquiring about your product or service before too long.

There's a fellow you may be familiar with named Joe Girard who holds the honor of having sold three times more Chevrolets than anyone else on earth. Joe made a single, breathtaking discovery—and that discovery is what made it possible for him to become a true sales superstar.

Joe Girard found out that 100 percent of the people he came in contact with would eventually either need a car or be able to introduce him to someone who did.

Think about that. If that piece of information is used correctly, the consequences are staggering! It means that every car Joe sold was more than just another sale. It was a doorway to a new customer—and, as if that weren't enough, a doorway to still another doorway! And the same went for every single new person Joe met—whether or not that person decided to buy a car!

The potential for developing your customer base by using this approach should be obvious. Let's say you sell a widget to Mr. X on a contract that's good for the next three months. Now, if you keep in contact over the weeks with Mr. X (and I believe you should), that's three months of interaction not only with Mr. X but also with any acquaintances he'll be willing to refer to you!

Similarly, if Ms. Y, whom you met recently at a party, doesn't use widgets in her operation, but knows all sorts of people who do, there's no law against asking her, tactfully and professionally, if she knows of anyone who might benefit from your product. If she supplies you with a couple of names, and gives you permission to mention the fact that she suggested you call, you know what you've got? You've got the kind of leads salespeople kill for, that's what you've got!

Tool number four: Your Filing System

Of all the organizational tools available to you, by far the most powerful is the Prospect Management Board.

What's powerful about it? It's simple; it's visual; it's direct; and it tells you what you need to know. There's a sample board on page 35.

As you can see, it gives you instant information on the status of your accounts.

Viewed in detail, the board might look something like the one on page 36.

Take a close look, because you will want to duplicate this information on your own prospect cards. Each box represents an index card with the essential information about each of your prospects printed on it. (The dollar figures in the upper-right-hand corners represent your estimate of the value of the account. This information, while perhaps

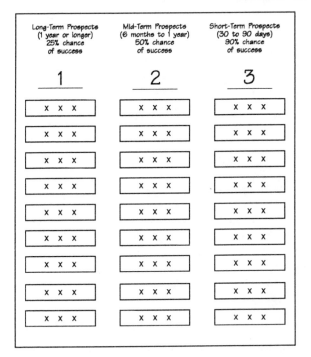

Long-Term Prospects (1 year or longer) 25% chance of success	Mid-Term Prospects (6 months to 1 year) 50% chance of success	Short-Term Prospects (30 to 90 days) 90% chance of success
1	2	3
x x x	x x x	x x x
x x x	x x x	x x x
x x x	x x x	x x x
x x x	x x x	x x x
x x x	x x x	x x x
x x x	x x x	x x x
x x x	x x x	x x x
x x x	x x x	x x x
x x x	x x x	x x x

not accurate in the minutest detail, can be a powerful motivator!)

The cards are grouped in columns according to where each prospect is in the sales cycle. Those in the first column, for instance, are less likely to close. At this stage, the chance of success is only about 25 percent within a year or more. However, your objective will be to move them to the next step. These prospects will need a lot more attention before you can make the sale.

Prospects in column 2 are somewhat closer. You have about a 50 percent chance of closing the sale within the sales cycle. (All of these percentage estimates are "ballpark" guidelines that may vary a few points from industry

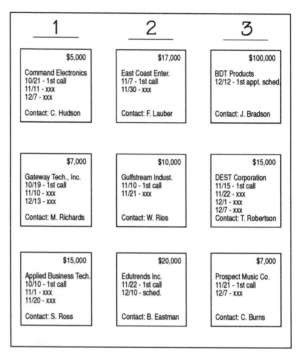

1	2	3
$5,000 Command Electronics 10/21 - 1st call 11/11 - xxx 12/7 - xxx Contact: C. Hudson	$17,000 East Coast Enter. 11/7 - 1st call 11/30 - xxx Contact: F. Lauber	$100,000 BDT Products 12/12 - 1st appt. sched. Contact: J. Bradson
$7,000 Gateway Tech., Inc. 10/19 - 1st call 11/10 - xxx 12/13 - xxx Contact: M. Richards	$10,000 Gulfstream Indust. 11/10 - 1st call 11/21 - xxx Contact: W. Rios	$15,000 DEST Corporation 11/15 - 1st call 11/22 - xxx 12/1 - xxx 12/7 - xxx Contact: T. Robertson
$15,000 Applied Business Tech. 10/10 - 1st call 11/1 - xxx 11/20 - xxx Contact: S. Ross	$20,000 Edutrends Inc. 11/22 - 1st call 12/10 - sched. Contact: B. Eastman	$7,000 Prospect Music Co. 11/21 - 1st call 12/7 - xxx Contact: C. Burns

to industry. In my experience, however, they are generally valid figures.)

As for the prospects in column 3, things are looking pretty good. You have a 90 percent chance of closing a sale within thirty to ninety days with these people.

Then, of course, there are the two invisible columns. To the left of column 1 is your list of cold calls. These are the prospects-to-be. Your goal is to move them into column 1, to get them into the sales cycle.

To the right of column 3 are your customers, the prospects who actually closed a sale with you. Your goal is to replace each one, each successful sale, with *two new prospects*.

This step is crucial! You may have five prospects in your third column, but if you have only one in column 2 and none in column 1, there's trouble ahead. You're going to run out of sales—and income.

Let's assume for the sake of argument that the normal sales cycle is ninety days. (Again, in actual practice this may vary from one industry to another.) If you have to start the whole process over from scratch *after* you complete a sale, you'll have to wait another ninety days for your next paycheck!

The point is, you must keep the process going. Prospect. Make your sales calls. Move the cycle along. Your three columns should be about equal to ensure continual success—and continual income.

Let's take another look at our three categories. Remember, your goal at every stage of the sales cycle is to move the prospect to the next stage.

A "1" prospect will need a considerably greater investment of time if you are to move him or her along to the "2" level than a "3" would need to get to a signed contract. Still, a "2" client needs to be worked constantly to get him or her to the "3" level.

To put it another way, all three categories of prospects represent money to you *eventually*—it's just a matter of when.

A note of warning: you must be brutally honest in categorizing the prospects, and you must use your own experience to fine-tune your categorizing efforts on an ongoing basis. A "1" client who has been a "1" client for three months is about as useful to you as a beached whale.

Put your Prospect Board in a prominent place in your office where you will be sure to see it every day. You will never again be surprised by what's happening to your client base. You'll be able to see graphically exactly where you are and what you have to do.

The system really is incredibly effective. Forget the special logbooks, forget the computer programs. They don't work in managing prospects. Of course, if you have a hundred current *accounts* to keep track of, by all means use a computer. But for your new business, either with an old client or a brand-new one, the Prospect Board is the way to go. It keeps leads from falling through the cracks and ensures that you will not fall victim to the natural ups and downs of the sales cycle.

Tool number five: Your Initiative

Sales, perhaps to a greater extent than any other professional occupation, demands a great deal in terms of individual initiative and the ability to motivate oneself. Now, when most people hear the word "motivate," their eyes glaze over a little bit: here comes a lecture about how important it is to get in to the office on time in the morning.

When I talk about motivation, I mean taking on the responsibility to affect your environment in such a way that your sales efforts will be more profitable for you. Period.

Because that's what it really comes down to. Your success. The beauty of sales as a profession lies in the fact that you control your own destiny. Nobody else is talking to your clients, presenting your product, taking down your orders. And the degree to which you allow outside forces to determine your rate of success as a salesperson, in my book anyway, is the degree to which your initiative has failed you.

Recently, as one of my seminars was drawing to a close, I was talking to a salesperson about his approach to his job. It was in the middle of the summer.

"It's a tough month to sell, August," he told me. "Once we head into the fall, I'll do all right."

I hear this sort of thing quite a bit, and usually I'm quite diplomatic about how I respond. After all, a lot of businesses are seasonal (though this salesperson's wasn't). But this time I let him have it. Tough month for diplomacy, August. I think the heat probably got to me.

"It's true," I said. "August, everyone's on vacation. Can't sell during August, can you? You know what, though, a lot of the decision makers save up their vacation time and go in September. Who knows where they go, but it seems like they sure aren't in the office. So you can't sell in September. Then there's October. God, I hate October, don't you? Everybody's mind is filled with football and the World Series. You really can't get anything accomplished in October. Then there's November. Half the offices quit early for Thanksgiving; you've got the longest long weekend of them all right there. November—write it off. Then—watch out—HAPPY HOLIDAYS! They're all out shopping, drives me nuts, but you sure can't get any sales in December. January, It's off to Jamaica or Club Med or wherever they find to go, so you can't get any selling done in January. February, the darned MONTH is short on days, so what do they do? Stuff it with three-day weekends, that's what! March, the weather's so foul, who wants to go on appointments. When April comes around, nobody wants to talk business—they all want to take advantage of the nice weather they haven't seen for months. Same thing for May. June is okay, you can get in the door, but you'll always hear, 'Wait till after the quarter's over, we'll have a better idea then.' I don't like June too much, to tell you the truth."

"July's all right. I guess we have to wait a year to make our money, huh?"

Sending yourself negative messages like, "August is a tough month to sell" takes events out of your hands. Sending yourself positive messages like "Today is a great day to sell!" puts you right back where you belong: in control. Tough month or no tough month, August or no August, there you are with a job to do. Whose show is this anyway? Yours? Or August's?

Initiative, persistence, drive, motivation—whatever you want to call it, it's essential. It's that little voice in the back of your head that tells you you can do better than average . . . and that you have to. That you don't have to take anything for granted, even if everyone else does. In short, that you take responsibility for your own success.

Getting started

Now that we've had the chance to review what you'll be using, it's time to take a look at the environment you'll be working in. In our next chapter, we'll take a broad look at the entire sales cycle and offer some special hints to those salespeople who make their living on the telephone.

SUMMARY
Chapter Two: The Tools

✔ The fundamental idea behind any product or service is that it fulfills the need or desire of a given customer.

✔ It is absolutely impossible to make a sale to Company X.

✔ However, you can make a sale to John Smith, a fellow who works there and has a problem you can solve.

✔ Your first tool is your product; know it intimately.

✔ Your second tool is yourself; you must therefore be aware of the challenges and opportunities that accompany the unique set of skills and impressions that make up your professional image.

✔ Your third tool is your personal contact network; work to expand it. Tell everyone what you do, every chance you get.

✔ Your fourth tool is your filing system; it should be accessible and well organized. Consider using a prospecting board.

✔ Your final tool is your initiative; take the responsibility to affect your environment in such a way that your sales efforts will be more profitable for you.

Chapter Three

An Overview of the Sales Cycle—and Some Tips on Selling Over the Phone

Working in stages

Every sale can be broken down into four separate stages: qualifying, interviewing, presentation, and closing.

In this section of the book we're going to take a look at how the whole cycle can work, and the best ways to use the cycle to your advantage if your job requires that you complete all four stages over the phone.

Throughout the rest of the book, the focus will be on in-person selling. Looking at the telemarketing aspects, however, as we'll be doing here, is not only helpful to telemarketers—it's also a very good way to pick up the essentials of how the whole cycle works.

The only meaningful distinctions between the techniques used in an in-person visit and an over-the-phone "appointment" are in application. As you'll see, the basic principles will apply to just about anybody who sells something for a living. Things tend to get compressed when you're trying to make sales on the phone, though—which is why I've chosen to use this setting for our first walk through the cycle.

Because the steps I'll outline below may well take

place in a single telephone conversation, each step will concern itself with a portion of one hypothetical call. Of course, some sales may require a number of calls before you reach the close, just as someone who goes to see a client in person may very well have to make more than one visit.

Your objective: move on

Each stage of the sales cycle is meaningless outside of the whole process. That means simply that the objective of the first stage is to get to the second; the objective of the second is to get to the third; and so forth. There's no way you can do any one step independently of the others.

No matter how well or how badly you think the entry into or out of a stage has gone, the task at hand is to move, step by step, with your prospect, toward the next stage. You don't want to rest on your laurels or go back and redo work you've already done—you simply want to identify accurately the stage you've reached and, once you and the prospect are both comfortable enough with the idea, to progress and move ever closer to actually helping the prospect with your product or service.

This is what happens in each of the four stages.

Stage one: Qualifying

This one sounds like the easiest of the four on paper, but it can often be the most trying in real life: you and your contact determine that you're mutually interested in proceeding to the next step. That doesn't mean that you're positive the individual on the phone wants to buy your product or service—that occurs only in the fourth stage, Closing. Here, we're simply verifying that the contact is willing to discuss the potential usefulness of the product or service. In addition, we're confirming that the individual or company in question is the kind of account we would like to do business with.

That's a point beginning salespeople often overlook. The objective is not simply to hear the word "yes" over the phone. Your job here is to qualify leads. Let's face it—there are some strange people out there. Every once in a while you're going to run in to someone who's not worth wasting time on. Take responsibility for your calls, and think twice if you have good reason to believe someone's being less than forthright with you.

In this part of the cycle, we're overseeing the contact's transition from "suspect" (someone who may or may not be able to use the product or service) to "prospect" (someone we've determined could develop an interest in learning more about what we're selling).

Some salespeople are so frightened of the first stage (it's where most of the obnoxious rejections take place) that they try to circumvent it entirely. The idea is usually that you can find some sort of shortcut around the first stage by obtaining "hot" leads. While it's true that you'll generally have an easier time converting your leads if they're qualified to some extent, (rather than, say, ripped out of the white pages of the phone book), the fact remains that you're still going to be talking to someone you've never spoken to before. No matter what the statistics say about the contact, he or she must still make the all-important transition from stranger to valid prospect. In the real world, no list of leads is "prequalified"—someone, somewhere, has to make the effort to contact the person and say, "Hey, can I ask if you use fraxilators out there?"

During the first stage, you want to turn Mr. or Ms. Suspect—who's never talked to you before—into a prospect.

What should this first step actually sound like in a conversation? Here's an example of how it might go, though we'll be examining this step—also called "prospecting" or "cold calling"— in much more detail in a subsequent chapter. The individual approaches will vary, but the qualifying conversation with the suspect (which happens, as you might imagine, once we've gotten past the front desk, and perhaps even obtained some information about the company) could sound something like this:

Suspect: Hi, Mr. Suspect here.

You: Hi, Mr. Suspect, this is Sam Smith from the United Fraxilator Corporation. I'd like to ask you something about your fraxilator service, if I may.

Suspect: Hold on, hold on. Let me stop you right there, Sam. I really have no interest in discussing our fraxilator service.

You: Okay; well, you know, Mr. Suspect, a lot of people tell me that at first, before they have a chance to discuss with me some of the benefits of the program we're offering. What I'd like to do if I could is ask just a couple of quick questions. Is that all right?

This turnaround constitutes the single most effective method I've come across for handling most of the objections salespeople face regularly. You'll find that it works at just about any point in the sales cycle. We'll be examining how it can be used most effectively later on in the book.

Suspect: Well . . . okay, I'll give you two minutes.

As you might imagine, the information that follows in such a conversation is very important—and marks the passage from the first to the second stage. Once you learn that Mr. Suspect does in fact have time to discuss fraxilators, he may fit your profile of a potential fraxilator user, and the fact that he said he had no need to discuss the product at the beginning of the conversation is less significant. We can start to think of him as Mr. Prospect, instead! By the same token, if the exchange I've just described finishes up a little differently, say, like this:

You: . . . What I'd like to do if I could is ask just a couple of quick questions. Is that all right?

Suspect: No. Leave me alone. Goodbye. (Hangs up.)

Guess what? Your contact is not going to be a prospect. When you started the conversation, he lived up to his name, and was a suspect, but he sure isn't one now. It's part of the cycle, as we'll see a little later, for there to be a few "no" answers along the way. For now, keep your perspective during calls like that one, and try not to let it affect your future prospecting work.

Let's summarize what we've seen here. It's actually quite simple. The goal at this qualifying stage is to determine that someone we've contacted has agreed to go through the cycle and discuss the product or service with us. Often, this agreement is unspoken or implicit.

Stage two: Interviewing

We find out the needs of the individual in order to determine what we'll say later on. This process can be compared to an in-person interview in the kinds of sales you'll find discussed elsewhere in this book.

The facts you gather will allow you to pinpoint the specific items that you're going to be offering your prospect. At this stage, typically, there are three basic questions, with two optional variations, to ask. Before you start asking them, you'll want to make a smooth transition, and offer your prospect the chance to learn a little bit more about you.

The three major questions concern the past, the present, and the future. The variations have to do with how and why. The full matrix of questions will be outlined in the later chapter on the interview stage; for now, we'll stick with the basics.

Prospect: Well . . . okay, I'll give you two minutes.

You: Mr. Prospect, let me tell you a little bit about us. We've been in business for the last eight years, and we happen to be the world's premier fraxilator company. And today I was just curious to find out a few specific things about your company's fraxilator use.

Prospect: Shoot.

You: Okay. Have you ever worked with United Fraxilator before?

Prospect: Well, yes, once we did, back in 1988. As to how it worked out . . . I can't recall any problems with it whatsoever, to tell you the truth. A couple of years after that, of course, we had some budget cutbacks; you know how it is . . . eventually we re-established our fraxilator service, though.

You: Uh-huh. And, as far as fraxilators go, what are you presently using?

Prospect: Well, at this point, we're using the old Cheap'n'Dirty, Inc. fraxilator, which isn't really that effective, now that I come to think of it . . .

You: Is that right. Tell me something; does your fraxilating department forecast much additional work over the next couple of months?

Prospect: You know, it's funny you should ask about that. I was just talking to Meg Powers over in Fraxilation this morning; she said that now that they've been assigned the new underfraxilation project, they'll be taking up most of our available fraxilator time, and we might have some delays.

Once you've gotten some ideas of your prospect's needs, you can consider moving ahead:

You: Now, that's interesting. You know, a lot of people working on the kind of project you've described typically find that we can help them with one of two types of fraxilators that I could tell you about. The first is our top of the line item, our model A-98.

Prospect: How much does it cost?

You: That runs a little over seven million dollars.

Prospect: Sounds kind of expensive . . . I don't think we could work that into the budget.

You: Hey, I understand. Well, the second one, the A-99, which also delivers superior results, is a little bit less expensive; it only runs eight dollars and ninety-nine cents. But it happens to have top-notch suction and great underfraxilation; it might be just what you needs.

Prospect: Hmm . . . that could work out.

The second stage will often terminate with just such an affirmation on the part of the prospect, a "that could work" kind of reaction, allowing you to move on to Presentation.

Stage three: Presentation

The sale has not closed.

This stage is where we supply more specific data about the benefits of our working with the client. Be careful not to assume that a successful interview indicates a progression to the final stage of the cycle.

Think about it. We now know two things: the person we're speaking to is in fact a prospect, and he or she has agreed that the product or service might have an application. That's it. We now proceed in a calm, professional, tone to the highlights of the product or service.

Features, benefit, proof

That's all very well, you may be thinking of yourself. But what, exactly, should you say?

There are many things you can discuss with the prospect at this point, but really, the only items of any significance can be broken down into three main areas: features, benefit, and proof.

A feature of the A-99 might be that it's easy to install. A benefit would be that it lets the user increase production (and not that it has, say, a very high fraxis retrieval ratio—that would be another feature). And proof of the A-99's effectiveness could be the fact that it was singled out for an industry honor by a trade magazine.

Now, all three ideas are important, but of most immediate interest to your prospect (who is, we are assuming, not speaking to you face-to-face) is benefit. (As we'll learn, proof tends to carry more weight during an in-person presentation.) Some salespeople confuse the customer benefit with either of the other two concepts. Features and proof are important, but what your prospect really would like most to hear about now is how the product or service you're offering will actually help him or her.

It follows, then, that you must know exactly what the benefit of your product or service is and be able to discuss it at the drop of a hat. With that in mind, let's examine how benefit differs from features and proof. Consider other things people buy. Why do they purchase them in the first place? Consider something as common as . . .

Green rubber boots. Why would a person go to a shoe store and pay for a pair of green rubber boots? What would that person really be buying? Let's think of the problem solved by a pair of green rubber boots. You're stranded at rush hour in front of a shoe store. It's raining furiously. You're wearing a pair of tennis shoes. You look in the window and see a beautiful pair of green rubber boots. You decide you can afford them. You walk in and buy a pair. What have you really bought?

Two dry feet! That's the benefit of green rubber boots. That's what the shoe store really has for sale.

The "what" of the boots—the features, such as lining, soles, color—is important. The "why" of the boots—the proof, the fact that you've read rave reviews about this particular brand—is important, too. But when you come right down to it, neither of these carry quite as much weight as the actual results the boots deliver. What is the result *your* product offers?

What saves a customer money? Make his or her business more efficient? Creates more profit? Whatever it is, that's the benefit you have to offer. The benefit is not the same as how the savings, profit, or productivity is achieved. "How" is interesting—and possibly crucial to your prospective customer. But it's still not the benefit.

From the potential customer's perspective, the "to buy or not to buy" problem is resolved by appealing to a simple (and often unconscious) three-way analysis—a triangle, with the benefit at the apex.

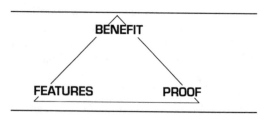

Benefit (you make it back to your house with dry feet). Features (waterproof lining). Proof (your Uncle Bert swears by these rubber boots).

After having outlined the benefit, we can advance to

the supporting concepts of features and proof. Here's how it all might sound when brought together.

You: Mr. Prospect, let me tell you a little bit about the A-99. (Benefit:) It will help you increase production by as much as one-third. (Features:) That's because it requires less maintenance, it's easy to install, and it has the highest suction rate of any fraxilator in its class. (Proof, part one:) It also happens to have been selected by Fraxilators Monthly as the top fraxilator of 1993.

This alone may or may not be enough to sway the prospect; accordingly, we must be prepared to bolster our presentation with another dose of proof. (People proof, if you will.)

You: Mr. Prospect, let me give you an example of how other firms like yours have been able to use the A-99. Bruce Singleton at Blue Ribbon Typewriter Corporation uses the A-99 exclusively, and has told me he will never purchase another fraxilator from anyone else. Frankly, I think this is an item that could benefit your company dramatically, as well.

Wouldn't it be great if, at this point, the prospect always responded by asking for details on when he could receive 5,000 A-99s?

Unfortunately, it doesn't always work that way. After

our initial discussion of what the product has to offer, we can expect to hear some objections. Though we've already briefly examined one of the most powerful turnaround techniques (the "other customers told me the same thing" approach), the topic of turning around objections is probably one of the most vexing you'll encounter as a salesperson. The problem really can't be addressed in full in this short summary. That's why I've devoted an entire chapter to it later in the book. Whether you sell in person, on the phone, or using two tin cans and a piece of string, you'll probably want to go over that information carefully.

It's no secret that the way you approach objections will, in large measure, determine how successful you will be as a salesperson. It will also have a tremendous influence on how often you progress to . . .

Stage four: Closing

This is where the rubber hits the road. If you've really been working with your prospect, being sure to listen every step of the way, closing is quite simple. If you've skipped a step, it's a nightmare.

You should begin your close by asking the prospect how he or she feels about the product/service you've described in your presentation. If the answer is a negative one, you're not ready to close. Return to the presentation (or even interviewing!) stage; do not pass GO, do not collect $200. If the answer is a positive one, and it's clear that the prospect feels there's a good chance of a match between what you're offering and his or her needs, it's time to formalize your arrangement.

You: Well, Mr. Prospect, how does what I've outlined about the A-99 sound to you so far?

Prospect: I'll tell you the truth, Sam, it doesn't sound half bad.

You: That's great!

One brief note here of special interest to those who sell on the phone: phrases like "that's great," "fantastic," "that's good to hear," and so on are important tools. Because you don't have the advantage of a person sitting in front of the prospect during a face-to-face interview, you have to reinforce every positive reaction you hear. Once you do, you'll find yourself engaged in a lot fewer dead-end conversations. These "reinforcement phrases" are useful at all four stages, but are particularly crucial during any attempt to close.

We now enter into the most crucial few seconds of any sale. I suggest you use a revolutionary closing technique, one we'll be talking about quite a bit a little later on in the book.

It's called asking.

Ask for the sale. *Ask* when you can get started. *Ask* if there's any reason you can't get the paperwork started now, today, during this phone conversation. *Ask* for the business.

You: That's great! Well, let me tell you what I think we should do. I'd like to get the paperwork started here so we can deliver 250 of the A-99s to you by the first of April. Does that sound good?

The above is an example of what I call "assumptive selling." We assume that the sale is going to close, and we focus on some of the details on that sale, rather than the existence of the sale itself.

Obviously, you can expect to hear something besides, "Yeah, Sam, let's go," after an assumptive close attempt. Here, as at any other stage, objections will arise. Again, you have access at this point to a very powerful turnaround—you'll see it in action once again in the dialogue below.

Prospect: I don't know, Sam. We've had a lot of trouble getting results out of the programs like this one.

You: You know, Mr. Prospect, it's interesting to hear you say that; I'll tell you why. I was just talking to the purchasing agent over at DJT Company a couple of months back, and he had the exact same concern. The fact is, though, they did place the order with us, and they're very happy with what we've done for them.

Now that you've responded effectively, don't let yourself lose momentum! Pick up where you left off:

You: So what do you say? I can get the shipping department rolling on this, and we can guarantee you delivery by the first of April. How does that sound, Mr. Prospect?

In closing, once you've laid the right groundwork, the best approach is always to *ask* for the sale.

All selling—and particularly selling over the phone— is a numbers game. Your numbers won't look great if you take a lackadaisical approach to getting the orders. Work with the prospect. Understand his or her needs. Listen. Cooperate. Then *ask* to get things started. Don't beat around the bush.

Of course, the beautiful thing about selling over the phone is that, if you get shot down, all you have to do is pick up the phone and try again. You haven't driven forty miles to meet the prospect. And as we'll see, every single one of those calls that doesn't work out is really working in your favor, because you have to hear a certain number of "no" answers before you get to a "yes."

Again, keep things in perspective; it's all part of the cycle. You can always pick up the phone and try again from square one.

In-person selling: where it starts

Well, that's the whole cycle in a nutshell. While the above analysis will be extremely useful for those engaged in telemarketing, it doesn't really contain enough detail to see you through all the subtleties that can confront you during in-person interviews.

Because of the many variables that present themselves during in-person meetings, they demand a much more thorough treatment. Accordingly, we'll turn our attention now to learning about each stage in depth.

And one of the things we'll learn is that, when it comes to in-person selling, the best place to start is (ready?) right in the sales office, in front of your telephone.

SUMMARY
Chapter Three: An Overview of the
Sales Cycle—and Some Tips on
Selling Over the Phone

✔ The four stages into which every sale can be broken down are: qualifying; interviewing; presentation; and closing.

✔ The objective of the first stage is to get to the second; the objective of the second stage is to get to the third; the objective of the third stage is to get to the fourth.

✔ In the qualifying stage, you will determine whether or not your contact (the "suspect") is interested in discussing the product or service with you, and moving further through the cycle. If this interest exists, the potential customer becomes a "prospect."

✔ In the interviewing stage, you'll find out the needs of the individual and how you can fill them.

✔ In the presentation stage, you'll supply specific information about the benefits of your product or service. Be careful not to assume the sale has closed at this stage; it hasn't. During the presentation stage, you'll discuss your product's features, benefit, and proof.

✔ In the closing stage, you'll proceed to ask for the sale—once you've learned how your prospect feels about what you've outlined about your product.

Chapter Four

Qualifying

Warming up to cold calling

The most effective form of qualifying (otherwise known as "prospecting") is called cold calling, and most salespeople dread it.

As we've just seen, cold calling is when the person on the other end of the line has no idea who you are, and you have no idea whether or not the person you're speaking with has an interest in your product or service.

It's true that phone prospecting will probably never head your list of favorite things to do. Cold calling is often maligned . . . but very rarely is it properly understood. The fact is, this stage of the sales cycle doesn't have to be a chore, and it doesn't have to be combative or aggravating for either the caller or the person being called. In my view, it happens to be the one element of anyone's sales work that's most likely to turn a lackluster performer into a superstar—and it can do so with extreme cost-efficiency. In this chapter, we're going to find out how.

Square one

Most salespeople who aren't engaged in telemarketing understand that you usually can't sell unless you talk to a prospect and make a presentation. It seems that very few understand that continuous prospecting is necessary to get in the door in the first place!

I recently had a discussion with a top insurance executive about his sales staff. The question we were debating was whether you had to be particularly brilliant to be a real superstar in sales—whether you had to, say, know computers inside and out to manage your contact list, or read volumes of trade publications every morning, or be able to out-jargon your product manager in describing the technical details of the product.

The answer, we both decided, was definitely "no."

The executive told me that he had dozens of very bright salespeople who simply seemed unable, despite the sharpest attitude and highest buzzword count in the office, to perform up to their full potential. On the other hand, there were others he'd have written off long ago who didn't seem quite as high-octane at first glance, but who nevertheless rang up stellar month after stellar month.

What was the difference between the groups? The first group didn't know how to prospect. The second group did. Simple as that.

You do not have to have a Ph.D. or speak computerese to make money—like nobody's business—in sales. What you do have to do is prospect. If you don't prospect, odds are you won't be in the position to close the higher sales volumes.

Prospecting is something the professional salesperson must do every day, day in, and day out—no matter how good the numbers look at the moment, no matter how many sales you closed today. Those who understand this simple principle are the ones who really stand to make the most out of their sales careers.

In this chapter, we'll examine a number of ways you can develop your prospecting efforts. This will include an in-depth look at how best to use that one simple phrase we encountered in the last chapter—a phrase that can turn around the vast majority of the objections you may encounter on the phone.

Twenty/five/one-two-three

Qualifying by phone requires a certain degree of tenacity—stick-to-it-iveness, if you prefer. That doesn't mean it requires an overaggressive, combative, tone—just a certain degree of self-confidence and the willingness to hear some "no's" before you get to a "yes."

Now, fortunately, that's pretty easy to do once you get an idea of the actual numbers involved. To help with that, I'm going to give you a formula that's been developed over years of work with literally thousands upon thousands of salespeople—it helps you get a little perspective on what you're actually taking on in your phone prospecting work. Here it is:

$$20{:}5{:}1/2/3$$

What does that mean? It means that, typically, a successful salesperson is going to need to speak with twenty decision makers in order to make five in-person appointments, and that, from those five appointments, he or she can expect to turn between one and three of them into sales, depending on individual rates of effectiveness and market conditions.

Remember, that's twenty decision makers. Conversations with receptionists and other intermediaries aren't included in this formula.

That formula, simple as it may look, carries tremendous implications. It means, for instance, that if your objective is to see fifteen people a week, then the odds are that you're going to have to call sixty people to get those fifteen appointments—the same four-to-one ratio that shows up in the 20-5-1/2/3 formula.

Moreover, it means that of those fifteen appointments, you're going to expect to close between three and nine sales on those appointments, depending on your own circumstances and environment.

The point of the formula—and this chapter, for that matter—is that the sales don't materialize out of thin air. They're dependent on the appointments, which are in turn dependent on the calls. That means that good phone prospecting techniques can (and should) be the cornerstone of your successful sales work. Once you fully understand this, my bet is you're going to agree with me that they should be part of your daily schedule, not a weekly or monthly task you put off until you can't avoid it any more.

The nineteen no's

It's time to look now at at another big implication of 20:5:1/2/3.

Let's be cautious and assume that you fit into this formula on the low end—that is, you'll close just the one sale after five appointments and twenty calls.

Now, believe me, that's a healthy little average. I know a lot of salespeople who've adopted this program and come in on the low end of 20:5:1/2/3 who are doing very, very well for themselves. That one-to-three variation is a function of any number of factors—what you're selling, the level of competition you're facing, the number of sales you make over time, that kind of thing. But, bearing in mind that every salesperson is different, let's assume that the work you'll do will fit in on the bottom end of these realistic standards—standards that successful salespeople can and do achieve in order to pick up real-life, hefty commission checks.

That means we're looking at twenty calls to five appointments to one sale, right?

Now, let's take a look at the overall cycle. How many "yes" responses do you ultimately get out of those twenty calls—as in, "Yes, I would like to buy your product"?

One.

How many "no" responses?

Nineteen!

Now we've already determined that this is a working average—a very realistic and workable goal for you to shoot for, this 20/5/1-2-3 business. What on earth does that say about the system if ninety-five percent of all the people you talk to ultimately turn you down?

It says that the "no" answer is part of the cycle, that's what it says. That when you talk to someone on the phone and they tell you they have no interest in what you're selling, that's good. That's to be expected. It's part of the syndrome, one of the nineteen "no" answers you're going to get on the way to your "yes" answer. The "yes" doesn't come until you hear the nineteen "no's"—so don't get frightened or angry when someone says no! On the contrary, you should welcome it as an integral part of the cycle!

This is an extremely important point, one you'll find will help you put forward the right attitude as you make your calls.

You cannot look at a list of twenty unqualified names and know which one is the one "yes." Moreover, you cannot look at a list of twenty unqualified names and pick up the phone and make twenty sales.

(Let me put a disclaimer on that last sentence. I can't unerringly pull twenty sales out of twenty blind leads, nor can anyone else I've ever met in my life. If you can, then you probably don't need this book, and you should give me a call to see about the possibility of working for DEI Management Group!)

So if you find that you're able to hit the 20:5:1-2-3 ratio (and most good salespeople can), and you decide you want to see those fifteen people a week, then you are going to have to call sixty people, every week you're a salesperson, forever. And I do mean forever, because those sixty weekly calls represent your pipeline of incoming prospects—and that's a pipeline you don't want to see run dry.

How you can close too many sales

What an idea! Closing too many sales! Is this man Schiffman off his rocker?

Not at all. Here's a story that will show you exactly what I mean. I worked recently with a very big company whose most successful sales rep determined that he needed only 250 sales a year. He reached a point where he had approximately 1,200 clients with whom he was working regularly. So he decided that all he had to do was go back and sell to those 1,200 contacts day in and day out—and he decided that he wasn't going to prospect. It was a big mistake.

Lo and behold, the years went by and things turned sour. Predictably, he'd done spectacularly at the beginning (as a result of prospecting he'd done in the past) and then, slowly, his performance—and his commission dollars—began to slip. His client base started to dwindle. For a while, he couldn't figure out what the problem was—but I'll bet you can.

By the third year he was in serious trouble. He was running out of prospects, and he realized, as time went by, that the chances of his returning to his original sales level . . . the one that carried with it all the vacations and the fat commission checks . . . was pretty slim. All of a sudden he had to work like crazy on rebuilding his client base. By that point it was something of a losing battle, and the superstar of the staff found he had dug himself into a very nasty-looking hole.

So—here's one big secret that successful salespeople tend to learn:

It is in the nature of any client base to
deteriorate.

No matter how well you're doing, how many smiles you pick up from your clients, how good it all looks today, you can't quarrel with this law any more than you can try to repeal the laws of nature or argue against the facts of demographics. After all, people die, companies go out of business, contacts move on to new companies. It's just part of the rules of the game.

That's where good cold calling comes in. Good cold calling requires that you have a working number of potential new prospects (suspects, I call them) every working day. Period. For example, in my business, I make fifteen cold calls a day—every day—no matter what. The results get transferred to a prospecting board I keep of about twenty-five active prospects. That board is always full, and my job is always to get fresh names onto it.

When you get hypnotized by the act of closing sales . . . when you convince yourself you have more customers than you could ever possibly exhaust . . . when you get so many sales that you decide you don't have to prospect . . . that's too many sales. That means you haven't learned to handle your sales cycle yet. That means it's time to rework your prospecting skills and reintegrate them to your daily efforts.

As you may remember from our discussion of tools like the prospecting board, someone moving off the list of possible customers, for any reason including becoming a customer, is cause for concern on your part and renewed determination in your cold-calling work. It bears repeating: you must always have prospects in your "pipeline." When I close a sale, it means (at one level), that I'm potentially in some trouble as far as my cycle is concerned.

Granted, I'm ecstatic that I have this new client. That's why I'm in business, after all! But what good is the new customer going to be to me if I'm out of business this time next year? Next year, I'm going to have to have a group of active clients and a group of hot prospects. Where will they come from? They'll come from the work I do today to replace the prospect that just left my board! From the point of view of straight mathematics, it's exactly the same result to my prospect base if the prospect leaves the board because he or she tells me "not interested" or if he or she tells me "great idea, let's start next week." The net result is, negative one prospect. I've got to put it back.

An asking game

Selling is an asking game.

There's a man who stands on 42nd St. in New York City who sells business-card cases. All he does, all day long, is stand there and hold up a case, saying, "wanna buy, wanna buy, wanna buy, wanna buy . . . ."

That's not really your textbook, business-school-recommended selling technique. Still, every day, there he is, chanting "wanna buy." And you know, he does sell those cases. Every five minutes or so, someone stops short, takes a look at what he's got, and gives the fellow his three bucks for a business-card case.

Here's my question for you—what do you think the odds are that there's somebody doing the same thing in the middle of the Mojave Desert?

Pretty slim, right? Hard to close a sale in the middle of the Mojave Desert.

It's interesting, too, that he doesn't stand there in front of the subway and say, "Ladies and gentlemen, we're all aware of the increasing importance of business cards in today's high-paced economy. The World Almanac estimates that there are forty-six million business cards printed every year in the United States, and perhaps more on a per capita basis in the Japanese and Western European marketplaces. This highlights the role of the business card in contemporary urban society. I ask you to examine its true role in your life. How important your business card is to those who meet you for the first time! And how essential the method of conveyance you select for it! I happen to have in front of me, ladies and gentlemen . . ."

Now, it is true that once someone walks by his corner, listens to a few "wanna buy's", and stops to look, he changes his tune. Then he answers the questions his customers have about the product. But the minute he's back on his own, looking into the crowd of commuters, it's back to, "wanna buy, wanna buy, wanna buy . . ."

So let's see what we've got. The "wanna buy, wanna buy" routine works in the middle of Times Square, but it doesn't work in the middle of the Mojave Desert. What's the fundamental difference between the two places? Forty-two million people! That's how many people walk through Times Square every year.

And the longwinded discourses on Our Friend The Business Card, if they show up at all, don't make an appearance as long as the main effort is still to identify new customers.

Our intrepid business card case salesman has learned a basic principle of good prospecting. From the point of view of qualifying new prospects—which is what cold calling is, remember?—a short, simple message to a whole lot of people is better than a long, involved message to a few.

I don't care what you're selling. If you went and stood in front of forty-two million people with a sign proclaiming, "I sell X," someone would stop.

Don't believe me? Go take a walk and stop in front of the first retail store you come across. What is that?

A retail store is nothing more than a person who's decided to go one better than standing on a streetcorner. He stands inside a building in front of a sign that says, "I sell X here."

Suppose it was you. Suppose you went to Times Square, and just stood there looking forlorn with your hand outstretched. Do you think anyone would put any money into it?

If you said "no," you haven't been to Times Square recently. It's estimated that one out of every twenty-five people who pass by such a person will give money.

Now let's say you get a little more sophisticated—you hold out a little tin cup instead of just stretching out your palm. Better results with that approach?

Sure. And if you took a big piece of cardboard, wrote the words "I NEED HELP" on it, and stood there with the cup, would your income improve? You bet. And if you added sound, and stood there wearing the sign, with the tin cup in one hand, and the bell clanging away in the other, you think you might do even better? Of course you would.

The more simple, direct, noticeable—and, for our purposes, since we're not trying to become lifelong panhandlers here—the more professional your approach during the prospecting process . . . the better your results will be.

Keeping it simple

A little earlier, we looked at a sample telemarketing call that incorporated a prospecting section. Now we're going to learn how to put together a customized cold-calling script . . . the sole purpose of which is to get you appointments.

Where most people go wrong in cold calling is in feeling they have to tell their contact, over the phone, about everything that the given product or service does. Or that they must go over the inventory status of every item in the company catalog. Or that they are bound to explain how many business cards were printed in Turkey during the first quarter of 1989.

Who cares?

Do you care about any of that when you receive a cold call? I'm serious. Ask yourself what your main objective is when you receive an unsolicited sales call.

Be honest. Isn't it to get off the phone?

Nobody plans a slot in his or her day to receive cold calls. And most businesspeople are, by definition, busy. So the first thing we're going to do in developing our cold calling technique is, *remember what the person on the other end of the line is thinking.* More than likely, he or she is going through a series of questions that looks something like this:

---

1. Who is this person?
2. Why are they calling me?
3. Is it important?
4. What does it have to do with getting my job done?

Now, before we go any further, I want to make an important point. There's a very good reason you should give what I'm about to say an honest try.

It works.

I promise, it really does. Don't follow my suggestions for any other reason than that. Try it—if it works, use it. And don't tinker around with it, once you've discovered that it works.

Nothing bugs me more than watching someone make "improvements" on something they haven't really tried yet or, worse, yet, something that's already delivering results. Try what I'm about to suggest. Then, if it works, stick with it.

Why does it work? Because the system is really based on *your experience*. Let's say you call me up on the phone and all you say to me is, "Hey, Mr. Jones, wanna buy a pen?"—I have to respond. Somehow. I can respond in a number of ways. I can hang up. I can wait for you to keep talking. I can say no. I can say yes. I can say, "Tell me more about it." And you know I can say, "I'm not interested." But I will do something. And once you've made a lot of calls over a long period of time, you'll be able to categorize the responses. You'll eventually become quite familiar with some of the standard responses associated with selling in your field.

With that in mind, and acknowledging that you know your own product or service far better than I do, I can promise you that there are some fundamental ideas that have broad application for cold calling in virtually all fields. Let's start constructing the prospecting script and take a look at how the basic elements come into play.

Our objective is to get the appointment. Nothing else.

That's what prospecting and cold calling is about—getting the appointment, identifying the prospect. It's not about closing the sale. That's what the appointment is for. Right now we're interested in qualifying the contact; here's how we're going to do it.

The first step in the cold call is to get the person's attention, and to identify yourself and your company. (Answering the question, "Who is this person?")

The second step is to give a reason for the call and identify features and benefits of your product or service. (Answering the question, "What does this person want?")

The third step is a question which will attract their interest and lock them into a conversation. (Answering the question, "Is it important?")

The fourth step reinforces the second, emphasizes

the benefits, and reacts to the objection—which doesn't take us by surprise—or any questions that may arise from the previous steps. (Answering—as we'll see in a minute—the question, "How does this help me?")

The fifth step concludes the call by asking for an appointment.

That's it.

Here's what it sounds like.

You: <STEP ONE>: Good morning, Mr. Smith. This is Carol Carey from the Salamander Group here in New York. <STEP TWO>: Mr. Smith, the reason I'm calling you today is to introduce you to our new sales training program, which can effectively increase the productivity of your sales staff. <STEP THREE>: Mr. Smith, are ya interested in having a productive sales staff?

Stop talking and wait for one of two things to happen. Here's the first thing that can happen:

Mr. Smith: Yes, as a matter of fact I am.

That's easy enough to react to, isn't it?

You: That's great! You know, Mr. Smith, I'd like to drop by your place and show you some of the things we can do for you. I think you'll really be impressed. How's Tuesday at 3:00?

On the other hand, most cold calls aren't going to be quite that easy. Most calls will probably proceed like this:

Mr. Smith: I'm going to stop you right there, Carol. We really have no need for sales training at this point in time.

Now, before we go any further, let me explain something that you probably already suspect. My work with salespeople indicates that when Mr. Smith says that—or any of the thousand variations on it that you come across in sales calls—odds are that he is not really saying, "Carol, I've had a couple of weeks to study this question. I've called meetings with all our top people, we've hashed the question out a number of times. We've done some demographic surveys, had an outside consulting firm analyze the data, and what we've come up with is this—for a company our size, with our kind of staff, and with our management structure, sales training is not for us."

My experience is that, underneath it all, it's far more likely that he's saying something like this: "Carol, I'm very busy right now, and I don't really want to talk to you, because I feel that the project I'm trying to complete is more important."

Note that it's very rare for you ever to hear either answer that openly. It's all under the surface. So what I recommend you do is make one more try, under the assumption that it's really Answer Number Two you're hearing.

The one phrase that will turn around most of your objections

Now, when, Mr. Smith tells you that he's not interested right now, what's your reaction to that phrase? Think about it. Have you ever heard anyone say to you, "I'm really not interested in that"? Of course you have. It's part of every salesperson's daily existence. Forget my studies. When it comes to "I'm really not interested," what have *you* learned in your experience as a salesperson? Let's say you're at a party with a bunch of friends. Someone introduces you to a salesperson—perhaps someone who's just getting started in a career in sales. The new salesperson strikes up a conversation with you, and, after exchanging a few pleasantries, he says to you, "You know, I had the strangest thing happen to me today. I was prospecting on the phone, and the fellow I was talking to told me that he didn't have any interest in using my service."

What do you say? If you've been selling for more than a week, you're not going to say, "Wow! That's a new one! Not interested, huh? What'll they think of next!" No. You'll probably give the new salesperson a knowing smile and say, "Hey, don't sweat it. That's what a lot of people have said to me—people I ended up selling!" Well, if that's the case, then, as we saw in the last chapter, there's nothing wrong with saying that to Mr. Smith.

Mr. Smith: I'm going to stop you right there, Carol. We really have no need for sales training at this point in time.

You: <STEP FOUR>: You know, Mr. Smith, other people in your industry have told me exactly the same thing before I had the chance to sit down with them and explain how our program can increase their sales effectiveness. <STEP FIVE>: I wonder if we might get together. Would Wednesday at 4:00 be better?

> *Mr. Smith:* Gee, Carol, it sounds interesting, but Wednesday is just no good. We have department meetings all day on Wednesday.
>
> *You:* Well, this Monday at 1:00 is open. How does that sound?
>
> *Mr. Smith:* Monday . . . hold on, let me get my calendar.

It works—so don't change it!

The technique I've just outlined—which many salespeople find a little brusque and fast-moving at first—can take a little getting used to. But it does have one thing going for it. It works. Try it. Tape-record your calls, and make note of the ratios you keep and the reactions you encounter in a spiral notebook.

You'll find, as thousands of the salespeople I've trained have found, that it works like crazy. The reason it works is that it doesn't incorporate an attempt to sell the product over the phone—it saves that for the in-person appointment.

That "all-purpose-turnaround" I've described, the one that goes like this:

> You know, Mr. Smith, a lot have people have said that. But once I had a chance to discuss how our program could help them, they decided to give our service a try. . .

. . . has the virtue of applying to virtually every objection you encounter regularly, at virtually any point in the sales cycle. But for now, it's most important as a tool for helping you schedule appointments. And scheduling appointments, for most salespeople, is what the qualifying stage is all about. Give it an honest try and you will see results. No one makes an appointment on every cold call, but my work shows me that you can expect a dramatic improvement in your prospecting work if you follow this technique.

And, wonder of wonders, what I'm suggesting you say really is true for virtually all salespeople. If people hung up the phone or walked out the door every time they heard the words "I didn't get your information in the mail," "I don't have time right now," "It's too expensive," or any of the other standard objections—then no one would ever sell anything!

Repeat, reassure, resume

This is an extremely effective technique. You'll get a better idea of its application in subsequent stages of the sale later on in the book, but for now, you should be prepared to use it in your cold calls.

Obviously, some objections may come up more than once over the course of a call. Instead of repeating yourself and sounding like a robot, repeat the prospect's words and sound like a pro. Reassure him or her that the concerns are legitimate but can be addressed to everyone's satisfaction, then keep going. Where appropriate, try to use the names of other companies or clients with whom you've worked. It might sound like this.

Mr. Smith: We've decided that we can't afford a new computer system right now.

You: Okay, so it's a question of cost?

Mr. Smith: Basically, yes.

You: Well, fortunately, that's a hurdle we usually don't have any problem getting over. As a matter of fact, Mr. Smith, MNO International, which I believe is one of your competitors, had exactly the same concern before they decided to go with us. How would you feel about getting together at 2:00 on Monday afternoon?

As you can see, this is really just a variation on the basic turnaround technique. (Of course, you shouldn't claim to have worked with Mr. Smith's competition if you haven't—adjust the script to fit your own sales history.)

Remember the numbers—and don't be a gerbil salesperson

What's a gerbil salesperson?

It's someone who goes round and round on a little treadmill for no particular reason. Gerbil salespeople get stuck in conversations like this:

Mr. Smith: I really have no interest in your service, Carol.

Gerbil: Gee, Mr. Smith, that's what a lot of my current clients said before they started to see how we could save them money in handling their payroll. What I'd like to do is come see you on Wednesday at 3:00—how does that sound?

> *Mr. Smith:* It sounds lousy. I don't want to save money. I don't want to talk to you. I don't want to restructure my payroll department, and that's that, okay?

> *Gerbil:* Now, why is it that you don't want to save money, Mr. Smith?

Please. Don't get me wrong. The conversation is going great, all the way up until our gerbil salesperson asks that stupid last question. Who cares why Mr. Smith doesn't want to save money? He obviously doesn't. He's taken the time and effort to tell us that he doesn't want to save money. Why spend valuable time we could be using to prospect better leads talking nonsense?

Questions like "Why don't you want to save money" polarize and inflame the exchange. The best approach is usually to make two tries to overcome an objection and set the appointment, then close out, say thanks for your time, and hang up. You may want to try more than twice, and you certainly are free to adjust the technique to your own setting and personal style, but remember that polarizing the conversation does neither you nor the prospect any good whatsoever. It just wastes time and gets you both mad. Remember the numbers: twenty decision makers turn you down fifteen times—five appointments turn you down four times—you close one sale—and you're doing great. Every "no" just leads you to the opportunity for another "yes."

Some final thoughts on qualifying

Here are some additional ideas that will help you through the qualifying stage.

Develop a script you feel good about—then stick to it. It

should probably be just as concise as the one I've offered here, but obviously you shouldn't feel constrained by a word-for-word "straitjacket."

Develop a spontaneous tone. This is very important. People don't react well to a call that sounds like it's coming from an automaton. Constantly review your calls: cold calls represent the portion of your selling cycle over which you probably have the most control. Monitor your work. How do you sound? What kind of responses do you get? What can you do to sound more "natural" and less "canned"? How can you best answer questions and concerns, then return from where you left off, without sounding as though you're reading from a manual?

Don't go overboard. Far too often, salespeople spend valuable prospecting time going into tremendous detail about the features of the product or service. Save that for the appointment. Try to follow the structure of the script I've provided—isolate a benefit (increased sales, for example, or higher production, or a more motivated staff), overcome the objection, then try to set the appointment.

Develop your personal script on paper first. That way you'll feel comfortable with it. Keep notes on the kinds of objections you receive and your personal prospecting ratios.

End with a question. Concluding appropriate sections of your pitch with a question (". . . don't you think?" "Is Friday at 2:00 all right?" "Are you interested in attaining higher sales levels?") keeps you in control of the conversation. Stay in control of the conversation if you can, and try not to use statements like, "I'll be in your area at the end of next week. When would be a good time to drop by?" That makes you sound unoccupied and unprofessional. Offer a specific slot in your schedule.

Keep the conversation short. Even if (especially if) the prospect sets an appointment. Set the date, then say thank you, see you at such and such a time on such and such a day, good talking to you, and end the call. *All you can do is set the appointment.* You can't close the sale now; attempting to do so will only lower your odds for completing subsequent stages successfully.

SUMMARY
Chapter Four:
Qualifying

✔ Effective qualifying (or "prospecting") is the one element of anyone's sales work that's most likely to turn a lackluster performer into a superstar.

✔ The most effective form of prospecting is cold calling.

✔ Continuous prospecting, on a daily basis, should be worked into your schedule.

✔ Typically, a successful salesperson is going to need to speak with twenty decision makers in order to make five in-person appointments; from those five appointments, he or she can expect to turn between one and three of them into sales, depending on individual rates of effectiveness and market conditions.

✔ For every sale you close, you can probably expect to hear nineteen "no" answers from your prospects.

✔ A short, simple message to a whole lot of people is better than a long, involved message to a few.

✔ When you speak with someone on the phone who is not expecting your call about your product or service, you can expect the following questions to run through the suspect's mind during the conversation:

Who is this person?
Why are they calling me?
Is it important?

What does it have to do with getting my job done?

✔ When, during a cold call, the suspect tells you there is no interest in your product, it's likely that he or she is in fact saying that he feels that your call is unimportant; in most cases, you can proceed under the assumption that this is the case, and make one more try to set an appointment.

✔ In doing so, you may want to appeal to the fact that "other people said the same thing before they worked with us." This turnaround has many applications beyond the qualifying stage.

✔ Repeat, reassure, resume.

✔ Don't be a gerbil salesperson.

Chapter Five

Interviewing

Whose agenda is it?

You've set the appointment. Now what?

During the entire sales process, but especially during the interviewing stage (which begins the moment you walk in the prospect's door), the single most important point for you as a salesperson to keep in mind is that the overall objective of the entire cycle is to satisfy the customer's needs. Not your needs.

You may want to win a sales contest that measures how many Model X Widgets you can sell over a one-month period. That's your goal. If the prospect's goal is to run his operation more efficiently through the use of features that are available only in the Model Y Widget, the contest takes a back seat!

The only goal that counts is the prospect's. You must now determine exactly what those goals are.

If you sell cars, the most important thing you need to find out about your prospective buyer is what he is looking for in an automobile. What kind of driving does he do? What kind of car is he looking for? What car would it be replacing? Is it a status-symbol car, a compact, a pickup? How will he use the vehicle? For long road trips or a short daily commute? All that information gives you sufficient insight into the individual prospect's profile to determine the proper vehicle to sell. You can't walk into that room with a long list of preconceptions.

It's very dangerous to walk into your first appointment waving around a sample of the Model X Widget (or any other specific item you expect the prospect to buy). Your goal during the interview stage is three fold:

- to obtain information,
- to provide information,
- and to inspire trust.

How on earth can you do any of that if you've already decided what the prospect has to buy?

Don't walk in the door with the sole purpose of talking about how great your company is, or what the Model X can do. You may be able to get to that later. For now, your main job is to *listen*. Not to sell.

When your choice of product or presentation method excludes the needs of the prospect, *you are wrong*, and you will almost certainly lose the sale. Now, before you can meet those needs, you have to determine what they are. Therefore, presenting any product right now is out of the question.

It would certainly be nice if you could just hand your prospect a questionnaire, or run down a list of predetermined questions, then head out the door. But human beings are a little more complicated than that.

Any social setting—and sales is emphatically a social undertaking—carries with it a certain amount of ritual. A good salesperson will understand the importance of making the prospect feel good about that crucial first meeting, and will use certain social rituals to his or her advantage. We'll learn how to do that with our first sales dialogues in this chapter.

What's not being said during the interview

Experts have concluded that 65% of our communication is nonverbal. That means, as many have suspected for some time, that when it comes to sales, it's not really what you say, it's how you say it. Your physical presentation is tremendously important as you begin the in-person phase of the selling process. If, at the outset of your appointment, you are going to be conveying some kind of nonverbal message to your prospect, whether you like it or not, shouldn't that message be: "I can help you"?

You bet it should. The prospect must feel great about you—and your product—throughout the meeting. That great feeling is essential to communicating that unspoken message of trust.

Perhaps the best way to accomplish this is to be sure that every conceivable scrap of upbeat, positive energy that takes place during the interview is reinforced and highlighted. One popular way to do this is to ask questions that are likely to receive a "yes" response—even on issues that seem unrelated to the purpose of your visit. "Yes" responses during the opening, "small-talk" section of a meeting are tremendously important in reinforcing the other nonverbal messages you'll be presenting with your handshake, attire, demeanor, and all the other visual and interpersonal "weapons" you possess.

Another important "weapon" that will once again come into play is the "people proof" we discussed a little earlier. That's where you say something along the lines of, "You know, we were just working with John Smith over at XYZ Company, and we were able to deliver such-and-such results."

This builds credibility, and can be an extremely powerful technique. However, I must caution you that there are two caveats that accompany "people proof." First, you must be certain to clear with John Smith (casually, perhaps) the fact that you may mention to prospective customers the fact that you've worked with him successfully. This usually does not present a problem. Second, you must be absolutely certain—especially where you're dealing with a potential competitor of John Smith's—not to reveal any information about Mr. Smith's business that might have the slightest sensitivity or have any proprietary significance whatsoever.

Those two cautions, of course, represent nothing more than a consistent and professional attitude on your part toward your clients and prospects, and should not hamper you in any significant way.

Personality differences: making them work for you during the interview stage

What's the best way to size up the personality type of your prospect—and use your assessment to help you project that positive, helpful image? Here are some pointers that will help you from the moment you walk in the door.

1. Look at the individual with whom you'll be speaking. Eye contact is vitally important in building any relationship, and yours with the prospect is no exception.

2. Adjust your speaking style to match the prospect's. If he's all business and doesn't feel like chatting, get right to the point and explain yourself a little more briskly than usual. If he's more easygoing, slow down a bit, and give yourself room to talk about non-sales topics so you can "ease into" the presentation.

3. Get a quick fix on the sort of person you're dealing with. Jung determined that there are four main kinds of communication styles. Just about everyone uses some component of each style; by the same token, just about everybody favors one style primarily in everyday life. Your job, as a salesperson, is to know

what category you use predominantly, as well as what category your prospect uses predominantly. Once you can make a good evaluation along these lines, you can alter your style so that it complements that of the person to whom you're speaking.

This information can be very helpful to you—but it's not a good idea to pigeonhole your prospects and base your entire interview on the premise that someone "is" one type. For one thing, you may not be seeing the whole picture in a brief in-person interview. For another, your energies are probably best directed toward building a common bridge of trust and open communication between you and your prospect; over-reliance on these categories may lead you into psychoanalyzing the prospect. Nevertheless, the broad guidelines Jung set out can be both revealing and helpful. Here are the four main categories. Where do you fit in?

Intuitors

Intuitors are creative, original, and can display quite a bit of charisma. They tend to show high levels of idealism, and can be quite effective when it comes to setting broad principles or far-flung goals. They can also exhibit unrealistic levels of expectation from those around them, and may run the risk of being considered removed from "real-world" events or capabilities.

Thinkers

Thinkers communicate precisely and efficiently, and can bring impressive amounts of intellectual ability to bear on virtually any problem. They are cautious and likely to explore all avenues before following a course of action. By the same token, they can run the risk of being perceived as icy or unemotional, and their insistence on "getting all the facts" may earn them the reputation of a person who can't make a decision.

Feelers

Feelers are dynamic, spontaneous, and lively; they are in touch with the problems and experiences of others and have a keen eye for personal values and loyalties. They rely on emotions to get their message across, and can be extremely persuasive. Their tendencies toward introspection may result in excessive guilt feelings; they can also be viewed as manipulative and oversentimental.

Sensors

Sensors trust their own experience base and not much else. They know what they want and don't mind using assertive or aggressive techniques to obtain their goals; a reputation for "getting things done" is usually their hallmark. They are typically positive, upbeat, and confident; they can run the risk, however, of appearing arrogant or overdominating in their dealings with others. They are sometimes criticized for not showing enough trust in others and not having a long-term view of the implications of their actions.

To a certain extent, these descriptions are stereotypes; but, by the same token, some stereotypes can supply us with valid insights if they're taken in the right context.

If the above communication styles don't seem to help you in identifying how you exchange information with the prospect, don't spend time trying to memorize them backward and forward. If, on the other hand, they seem to provide you with the "ammunition" you need to size up your prospect quickly, it might not be a bad idea to review the major points until you're familiar with the distinctive elements of each communication style.

The most important point, of course, is to use all the information and impressions you have at your disposal to help make the meeting progress smoothly. It may help you to appraise the communication style in combination with the reactions you receive from your prospect.

The prospect's reactions, too, are important signals, which you ignore at your peril. If your contact's eyes start to glaze over, for instance, something's almost certainly wrong somewhere; you may be throwing too much information out at once. On the other hand, if the prospect glances constantly at the clock on the wall and tries to speed you up with little "uh-huh" sounds, take the hint and get right to the point.

The first face-to-face encounter with the prospect

You've just walked into the prospect's office.

Quickly examine your surroundings. Try to find some part of the room that makes a statement about just who your prospect is—you'll be using that detail later. It could be anything: a statue, a photograph, a diploma, any kind of knick-knack at all.

Approach the prospect; reach out and shake the person's hands, looking him or her straight in the eyes.

Consider using an approach along these lines:

You: How are you? (Say your name.) Do you remember our conversation on the phone? (If no:) We'd agreed to meet today to discuss your (whatever) service.

Regardless of the answer to the question, proceed with:

You know, we just finished a program for another client just like your firm. (If possible and

appropriate, supply a company name.) Have
you people been busy today?

Sit down; wait for the prospect's reaction. In all likelihood, it will be something like this:

Prospect: Busy? Are you kidding? It's been a
madhouse. Who did you say you'd worked
with?

You: Well, I just worked with Mike Freehan
over at Joyride, Inc., and we did a very interesting thing over there. We were able to increase their effectiveness by 12 percent.

Prospect: Oh yeah?

You: That's right. Twelve percent.

Keep the initiative; now is when you comment on
your surroundings.

You: What a great office you have here. (Or:)
Gee, I love that painting. (Or:) Are those your
kids? (Or:) Look at that view! (Or:) Is that your
collection?

In other words, you retreat from the subject you just
brought up. Now, why do you want to do that? Well, what
you've done in the opening portion of the interview is to

establish some contacts and a little credibility. Now the objective is to make the prospect feel comfortable—by letting him upstage you. You decide to pick something from the environment that ties into the prospect's identity. Your next move is to find a way to let the prospect feel a little bit better about himself in discussing it.

Prospect: Yeah, those are mine—I collect miniature clowns.

Now: don't respond to this with some bland, expressionless reaffirmation of something you and the propect now both know. That is, stay away from the obvious: "Boy; that's terrific, miniature clowns." Instead. . .

You: I hear some collectibles are very hot investments. I worked with a guy once who collected Disney memorabilia. But he only had a couple of dozen pieces, as I remember.

Prospect: Well, I've been collecting these for about ten years; this isn't the whole group, by any means. I guess I have something like 2,000 at home. You should see 'em.

Obviously, this is all going to be of very limited interest to you if all you can do with it is present your product to people who have miniature clown collections. Here are some variations; remember that the goal is to get the prospect to relax, and perhaps get him to contribute a detail or two of his own. Then supply a parallel from your own experience base that doesn't look quite so strong by comparison with the prospect's.

Here are some more examples:

You: By the way, what did this building used to be?

Prospect: It was a factory. Used to make watches here.

You: Is that right? Well, the reason I mention that is, I go to quite a lot of offices, as you might imagine. But I don't see a lot of innovative thinking when it comes to work spaces.

Prospect: Well, I guess some people think an office building is an office building, huh?

You: But this place, you know, this is unique, it really is. So tell me, what do you do here?

You: Gee, you play golf, huh?

Prospect: Yeah, I do.

You: You know, I just got back from Scotchdale; I played out there.

Prospect: How did you do?

You: Actually, I didn't do too well.

Prospect: Bad day, huh? I just finished playing out in Bayonne and I broke a 100.

You: That's fantastic.

This example assumes a prospect who's a little less cooperative:

Prospect: Let me be honest with you about this meeting; when I scheduled this, I had no idea how crazy it would get around here . . .

You: Oh, believe me, I understand. Looks like you've got a full day today, huh?

Prospect: Yeah, I really am busy right now.

You: Now, it's interesting, the other day I was up in this part of town, and I talked to a group of people at Simmer Corporation; they were keeping busy, going through the motions, but I've got to tell you, it was obvious, they were pretty bored with what they were doing.

Prospect: Well, not here; boy, we don't have time to get bored.

You: Yeah, I can see that. Well, listen, I won't be long. . .

The objective is to create a common bond—something that we can talk about that isn't directly related to business. It can come from the surroundings, the level of activity in the office, the look on the prospect's face, any number of things. But you need to find out where that point of commonality is, quickly and smoothly, and then allow the prospect to assume a flattering stance on it over the first six or seven sentences you exchange. It may sound a little strange, but believe me, it works.

Let's take a look at another possible sequence. As you'll see, it follows roughly the same outline as the other scripts I've presented. Of course, there must always be some room for improvisation. Otherwise you're not making a presentation, you're reading someone an ad—and that's not going to get you anywhere.

YOU: Hi, how are you. John Smith.

Prospect: Anne Jones.

You: Do you remember our phone conversation?

Prospect: To tell you the truth, not really. . .

You: Well, I just finished a project—I think I mentioned it to you on the phone—we recently wrapped up a program with a company very similar to yours. And today I wanted to just tell you a little about it. Boy, you people are busy up here.

Prospect: We are. Actually, this has been an incredible year for us. We have never been busier.

> *You:* You know, I was over at one of your com-
> petitors' places a few months back, and
> some of the people there looked exhausted.
> Just exhausted. But I'll tell you the truth, be-
> tween you and me, I got the impression they
> don't like what they do.
>
> *Prospect:* Well, I really love it here.
>
> *You:* Yeah, I can see that. Hey, how long have
> you been here?
>
> *Prospect:* About ten years. . .
>
> *You:* How did you get the job?
>
> *Prospect:* Well, actually, someone called me
> up and asked me if I was interested in coming
> here.
>
> *You:* You're kidding. . .

"What can I do for you?"

Here's a very useful maneuver that will help you
avoid the trap of giving away too much information, too
soon.

> *You:* Hi, how are you, John? Nice to meet
> you; I'm Bob Smith.
>
> *Prospect:* Hi, Bob, come on in. Sit down.
> What can I do for you?

Believe it or not, responding to this innocent-sounding question is where many salespeople blow their best opportunities! *Do not* launch into your pitch—you haven't had the chance to interview yet. Retain the initiative by responding with a question of your own.

You: Well, John, you remember our conversation over the phone the other day?

Prospect: Not really—I know you do some kind of training.

You: Yeah, that's right. We do sales training and we just finished a program for Partridge Company, pretty similar to this operation, actually, and what we found out is that our program can be really effective for a company like yours.

Technically, you've now responded to the question—now, don't let any awkward pauses creep in! Keep the momentum, and remember that, during this interviewing stage, you want to get the prospect to talk about himself and/or his company.

You: Let me ask you a question. You look really busy up here. Is it like this all the time?

Prospect: Yeah, we really are swamped most of the time. We've got more jobs than we have hours to do 'em in.

You: Gee, that's fantastic. Now, Partridge was really busy, too—but, you know, they were losing prospects. The base was deteriorating; they weren't really working on getting the new clients when we got there.

Prospect: No, no, no, we know that we've got to get the prospects. We've got to keep going.

You: Hey, just out of curiosity, John, how long have you been working here?

Prospect: I've been here, let's see, it's almost fifteen years now.

You: Wow. Fifteen years, that's incredible. You must like it here.

Prospect: Yeah; and you know, part of the reason is, the people upstairs really give you a lot of flexibility.

You: That's great. One of the things that I notice at a lot of companies is that the communication between levels can sometimes be a little bit of a problem. People get stalled on a lot of things. It creates some problems.

Prospect: Well, here we have a pretty free rein to solve the problems. We can do pretty much what we want to do.

You: Hey, that's fantastic. Well, let me tell you something about us.

Now you're ready for the summary of your business—and so is your prospect. It's much more graceful to do it in the way I've just outlined than to dive into a "cold" lecture about your product or service. In the example above, it's only natural that the prospect should listen—it's your "turn!" He's told you about himself. . . now he's a little more willing to listen to you. Only after you've established a certain amount of trust can you launch into the next step: a brief summary of your company's work. That, in turn, will be followed by an in-depth discussion of the prospect's needs.

Here's another example of how to initiate the early exchanges of the interview stage.

You: Hello, Mr. Williams.

Prospect: Hi, Tom. Sit down.

You: Thanks a lot. Boy, have you ever got a great office here . . . !

Prospect: Yep; a lot of people tell me that.

You: You know, I was over at the World Trade Center the other day. I saw an office that had almost as much floor space as this one—but it sure didn't have this view.

Prospect: Well, the thing I like most about this office is that, on a clear day, you can see the Hudson River, sometimes all the way into Connecticut, too. There are times I think you can make out London in the distance.

You: Yeah, it's lovely. How long have you been up here in this office?

Prospect: Well, I moved in about six months ago.

You: No kidding. Where were you before?

Prospect: We were down at Ten John Street.

At this point in the meeting, you may consider using a nice little maneuver that will come in handy with a lot of the decision makers you meet. It's another technique for making the prospect feel good about himself before you get into the "real" questions.

You: Listen, just out of curiosity, what's your title here? What's the actual function. . . ?

Prospect: Well, in this department, we really handle the controlling aspects of the business, but our company makes sure we do a heck of a lot more than crunch numbers. When it comes right down to it, we're supposed to get out there and make the budget projections happen.

You: So you're the controller?

Prospect: That's right.

You: You know, I've got to say something. I've talked to a lot of people, a lot of controllers, and you know what? You really don't look like the controller type to me.

Prospect: (Laughs.)

You: You know what I mean? You look like you know what's going on.

Prospect: I do?

You: Just an observation.

Prospect: Well, if that's the case, that's probably because I'm usually the one who's got to make the decision.

The downhill interview

Now, I'm not going to play games with you. This approach to building rapport between yourself and the prospect is like everything else in sales—it's a numbers game. With some people, it will work spectacularly. With others, it may sound something like this:

You: Hi, Ms. Smith, how are you?

Prospect: Have a seat.

You: Thank you. Gee, you have a great view.

Prospect: What can I do for you?

You: Well, Ms. Smith, do you remember our phone conversation?

Prospect: No. Not at all.

You: Well, as I told you on the phone, we are a sales training firm. We've worked with about 200,000 salespeople, including XYZ Inc., one of your competitors. We've delivered some pretty impressive results. Boy, what a fantastic office!

Prospect: Yeah, it is nice. But what do you want? What can I do for you?

You: Well, as I told you, we are a training firm, and . . .

Prospect: 200,000 salespeople. Right. And?

You: And ah, I just wanted to figure out what you were thinking about working on in, um, in this area. . .

Prospect: I'm asking this just one more time. What can I do for you today?

You: Well, actually, the reason I called was to see if we might do a program together.

Prospect: No. We're too big.

You: Gee, we've been real effective for a great many of the larger firms.

Prospect: That's very interesting. We're not going to be one of them, though. Anything else? (Pause.)

You: What a beautiful office you have here.

Prospect: Yeah, I know.

That's a downhill interview. Statistically, there's not much chance of your pulling it out of the fire. It's a sobering experience, but it's worth reviewing. Don't assume every appointment will end in a sale. It won't. Your objective is to make the averages as favorable to you as possible. You have to be able to adjust to circumstances. Sometimes the sale won't come through. Sometimes it will.

I did a program at the head offices of an air express firm some time ago. I was discussing these sales dialogues with one of the salespeople, and she interrupted me and said, "Steve, don't get me wrong—this is a big help. But the fact is, the prospects don't know their lines." And she was absolutely right.

The reality of selling is that the prospect does not follow the script. In a way, you have to be ready to rewrite it (that is, you have to be familiar enough with the likely variations to adjust your strategy) on very short notice.

But that's the name of the game, isn't it? Remember, triple plays don't follow scripts, either. Bill Wambsgnass didn't stop in his tracks and bemoan his fate whenever the ball took an unexpected hop; he kept an eye out for the possibility of new opportunity. Then he let his instincts—his training—take over. You should strive for the same. With some prospects, you'll have success; with others, your exchanges may sound like the example above.

The first lesson is: be prepared for nothing to happen. Keep your perspective, and realize that every "no" is leading you to your next "yes." The second lesson is: be prepared for anything to happen. Once you get into the swing of things and you start making real contact with your prospect, you never know what may come your way!

Listening—and getting the facts straight

The next portion of the meeting will constitute the meat of the interview stage—describing your company briefly and getting the relevant information from the prospect.

In essence, all selling is really listening. Your focus must be on listening to what the prospect's needs are, and then finding a solution that is consistent with what you have to offer. As you spend more and more years in sales, you'll see that the salespeople who get to the top and stay there are the ones who see the act of selling as the process of solving customer problems.

Obviously, it is imperative that you know your product. You need to be able to explain the features of your product and discuss it in a distinct, interesting way. You can't do that if you're unable to answer fundamental questions the prospect is likely to ask (without warning) about your product.

The key to selling, though, is ultimately in determining what the client does and answering that by helping them do it better. Easier said than done, you may say. Yes, getting the particulars of a client's business can be a tricky business. A lot depends on the questions you ask, and later in the chapter, we'll look at that issue in detail.

Hard, easy—and everybody else

Our work at DEI over the years monitoring the interviewing skills of salespeople has demonstrated that there are three major categories into which members of any given prospect base will fit.

Typically, for instance, we've found that something like ten percent of all the people any given salesperson interviews will never buy—period. (Alas, we haven't yet figured out a way to determine exactly which ten percent that is before interviewing begins!)

Another twenty percent are what we call "easy buys." These are sales that really don't require that much effort on the salesperson's part at all.

The remaining seventy percent are the ones you really have to work on reaching during your interviewing discussions—the ones who could go either way. It's in developing this part of the prospect base that the real superstars emerge.

What's the secret? Listening has a lot to do with it; so does developing and capitalizing on the prospect's (well-founded) trust in you.

Trust

Sound simple? Well, believe me, it isn't. To be trusted, we have to become *trustworthy*. If you aren't sincere, you will not succeed. Period.

Not long ago, a woman in one of my sales training programs actually asked me, "Steve, can't I just appear to be trustworthy?" I'm going to assume that you know the answer to that question. To succeed as a salesperson, you have to be sincere in your interest in helping people. There's no faking that interest. Selling is a helping craft!

A can-do attitude

Hand-in-hand with trustworthiness goes the attitude that the customer's needs come first. You are there to help, and no matter what the customer says, you are going to find some way to do something for that person—even if it doesn't help you. "I can do that," you say, or "No, I can't do that, but I can do this."

A couple of months ago I was in a hotel giving a seminar. A hotel employee was setting up tables and chairs, and

I was getting things ready. I asked him, "Can you help get a bulletin board and some water?" Immediately, he put down the chairs he was carrying and went to get what I needed. A little while later I asked about a microphone. Again, he instantly put aside what he was doing and promptly called the audiovisual department. This man was pleasant at all times; he genuinely seemed to enjoy going out of his way for me.

Two weeks later I was at another hotel; I asked the employee there the same question. "Can you help me?"

"I can't," he replied. "It's not my job."

Which of these two do you think is going somewhere in life?

Nothing is going to win over a prospect like your willingness to be of service. I had a chance to demonstrate that attitude recently when a prospect told me he wanted to check out the competition before signing on with me. Without batting an eye, I gave him the names and phone numbers of the firms that compete with me.

Why did I do this? Two reasons. First, I showed that I was trustworthy. I was willing to let the client investigate my claims. Second, I showed that my prospect's goals were more important than my sale. I was there to help. This is what I mean by a can-do attitude. (By the way, I closed that sale.)

In praise of low-tech selling

Unfortunately, it's all too common that salespeople find ways to get around listening to the prospect and building trust. Over-reliance on computers is one of the most popular gambits, and seeing it happen makes me mad.

There's very little that gets on my nerves more, as a sales trainer and, yes, as a prospect, than to hear something like this:

"I'll tell you what I'll do. For this visit, let's just limit ourselves to the numbers. Then I can load all that information into our program and bring a printout with me next time I come by. That way the computer can show you what everything's going to look like."

What the hell does a computer have to do with anything? If the computer helps process information that you, Mr./Ms. Salesperson, want to pass along to me, Mr. Prospect, then make sure the information is perceived as coming from you. Not from a metal box. Why on earth would you try to get me to buy something based on something that comes out of a machine?

Sales is about people who trust other people. Period. I don't know who was programming your computer! All I know is you! Remember, I'm a guy in a room with a problem. I'm not a calculator. I have real concerns about how to solve real problems. I want to talk to a person—not a bunch of wires and glass and metal—who can help me solve that problem.

Computers have nothing to do with what you say to the prospect. (Unless, of course, you sell computers!) If you want to use a computer to prepare for a visit, fine, go ahead; if it makes you more productive, wonderful. But you can't expect a computer to build your relationship with the person sitting across from you. You can't forget for a moment that people buy things based on their emotions, and later justify their decisions with rationalization.

One more time. People buy things based on their emotions, then try to find intellectually sound reasons to justify their intuition.

That means the prospect has to trust you. Not a box

with a screen that blinks. You. It doesn't matter what the computer said. If the prospect can't trust you, you won't close the sale. You have to provide the prospect with sufficient one-on-one interaction to create an emotional bond that will justify a continuing relationship. If that doesn't exist, nothing's going to happen.

Now, you could say to me, "Steve, we've just sunk $4 million into a customized software program geared specifically toward new prospects; it's state-of-the-art. It illustrates exactly what their insurance needs are going to be over the next fifteen years. It's the greatest thing since sliced bread."

And I'd say to you, "That's great; throw it out."

For processing information, computers are fantastic. For making sales, they're completely inadequate. They do not provide prospects with what they're looking for: a place to put their trust.

As far as your sales calls go, forget about high tech. Go low-tech. Go one-on-one. Draw some pictures; take notes.

A little yellow pad

I'm absolutely serious. A little scribbled humanity on a simple legal pad with a ball point pen is, in most cases, far more effective than any amount of computertalk. Stay away from the printouts; stick with the yellow pad and a snazzy Cross pen. Proper use of these amazingly effective tools during the interviewing stage will help you build trust and foster better communication.

Taking notes can be a powerful sales tool. It reinforces the reason for your visit (to learn more about the prospect's problems), and it also helps you to listen. Perhaps most important, it puts you in a position of authority and control, and believe me, during the opening twenty minutes or so of most first-time in-person sales calls, you can use all the help you can get.

When I conduct my seminars, it never ceases to amaze me how effective the simple act of writing something down (in my case, on an easel) can be in encouraging communication. When I simply stand in front of an audience and ask, "What was good about the presentation we just heard?"—nothing happens. When I stand in front of an easel and write "Good points in presentation" and ask for suggestions on what should be listed—WHAM! The room comes alive!

If you write down notes during your interview, you're using three senses. Touch (that is, your hand, which is doing the writing), hearing (which is what you have to do to listen to the prospect) and sight (to see what you've written). My experience has been that these three sources of stimuli actually help you to strengthen your analytical abilities. By visualizing the facts and problems facing you and the prospect, nine times out of ten you'll find you're in a better position to come up with a solution.

Writing down details also sends very strong positive signals to the prospect, and you simply can't do that too much. When the prospect says, "I have 500 trucks, each of which holds 75 widgets, making deliveries 320 days a year," and then looks over and sees that you've written "500 x 75 widgets x 320 days/yr," guess what? You've scored points! You care! You're listening!

Use your pad as an easel—paint a picture for your prospect.

I'd suggest you use a standard yellow legal pad with a hard cardboard backing. It needs to be stiff enough for you to be able to write while it's on your lap. Keep your notes clean and spare; remember that they should be legible to both you and the prospect at all times. And don't doodle or make frivolous drawings for your prospect to appraise; it's unprofessional and makes you look nervous.

Where appropriate, use large diagrams in your notes

to underscore a point you're making verbally—and show your diagrams to the prospect. This can be an extremely valuable technique, as it pulls the prospect in to what you're saying, especially when you're talking about points that require some math or technical knowledge. Think about how much more accessible a discussion about insurance during the presentation stage might become if presented in this way:

You: So what we'd be talking about, Mr. Jones, is a benefit of $750,000 for your family in the event of your death. Now what we might do is ensure that 50% of that money, or $375,000, be put aside for your children's education, with the other 50% going into a fund paying 6% interest for monthly payout to your wife.

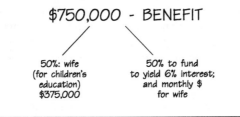

$750,000 - BENEFIT

50%: wife
(for children's
education)
$375,000

50% to fund
to yield 6% interest;
and monthly $
for wife

In the real world, where real customers are really bombarded with real overkill from increasingly unreal technology, that kind of accessible, high-communication, low-tech summation of a product or service can help you tremendously. More often than you'd expect, the prospect will breathe a noticeable sigh of relief and think, "Thank God! A human being!"

Care for a probing, Mr. Prospect?

Whatever weapons you've stocked your briefcase with, once you've established your rapport, fight the instinct to "lay it all on the table." As we've seen, the objective is simply to give a two- or three-sentence summation of why your company's fantastic, what it does, and how long it's been in existence, then (ready for the hard part?) stop talking.

See what happens. The next step in the process is to ask some questions, but before you do that, you want to be absolutely sure you're not steamrolling your prospect. So you wait and see what the prospect has to say at this point. It may be, "Gee, that's fascinating," or, "Please go on," or maybe even, "I really don't think your firm's right for us." Whatever the response, the prospect has to say something. Whether it's positive, negative, inquisitive, or indifferent, your next step is going to be to pick up the ball and start getting some information.

This part of the sale is frequently called the "probing questions" stage. Some sales books would have you look at it in just that way—probing. I prefer the term "interviewing" to describe not just this questioning section of the sale, but the entire in-person portion of the visit before the actual presentation.

Can you guess why I don't like to talk about "probing"?

If I'm interviewing you, I'm trying to uncover pertinent facts—facts that may be of benefit to each of us. Certainly that's the case in, say, a job interview, isn't it? While the experience may occasionally be a little nerve-wracking for the candidate, there's a goal toward which each partner in the process is working—learning whether or not a good "fit" exists, a strong enough pattern of mutual abilities and interests to justify a professional relationship together.

Isn't that really what you want out of the sales call?

Now let's change the terminology. Now I'm not interviewing you anymore. Now I'm probing you.

Be honest now. Doesn't that sound a little like you're dealing with an overaggressive interrogator in some prison cell somewhere? Or a police sergeant from a bad detective novel? Or a doctor you don't like very much?

Is that the right frame of mind for this very delicate relationship you're in the process of building up? Is that really how you want your prospect to think of you?

The "right" answers

Once you actually start to ask questions, it's a good bet that the individual is going to answer them in some form or another. But will the answers be short, curt, impatient ones? Or longer, detailed responses that move your visit along smoothly?

The goal is to get a good, solid exchange of information going. The more your prospect talks about the problem or problems that your firm can solve, the better your sales call is going, and the more leverage you'll have when the time comes to close the sale.

The $64,000 question, though, is, how do you keep the person talking? Most salespeople I meet tell me that the answer to that question is to keep asking questions—any questions. I'm not crazy about that approach.

For one thing, the information you need to get usually isn't that complicated, and I think that, once you get past the introduction, it's really a phenomenal waste of time to ask questions that have no real purpose. For another, asking questions doesn't mean a thing if you're using the questions as some sort of shield. The objective is to obtain information and build a relationship, and to do that you have to make sure that meaningful communication is taking place.

Regardless of what you're selling, my research indicates that there are three main areas of inquiry—past, present, and future—that you need to explore with a new prospect. Each of these three areas can be broken down a little bit further into a "what" and a "how" question, though how you approach these issues can vary somewhat from prospect to prospect. Here's what it looks like in matrix form.

WHAT?   HOW?

Past: What have you done in this area previously? How did you feel about it?

Present: What sort of service/product are you currently using? How does it work?

Future: What are your future plans in this area? How do you plan on accomplishing these goals?

That's it. That diagram covers, broadly, everything you need to ask at this point.

However, the manner in which you ask those questions, as you might imagine, is vitally important. Throughout the interview, the goal is to come across as a professional gathering facts. . . because that's exactly what you are! If you don't come across that way, you're asking for trouble. So don't hurry through the questions.

If you went to see the doctor because you had a stomach ache, how would you feel if your entire visit went like this?

You: Hi, doc. I've got a stomach ache.

Doctor: Stomach ache.

You: Right.

Doctor: Here. Take this pill. That'll be $75. Pay at the desk, please. Bye now.

You'd be upset, right? Because the doctor didn't ask you any meaningful questions.

He had no interest in you as a patient. He didn't even show you the slightest measure of common courtesy! You'd be extremely skeptical about your treatment.

Even if by some wild chance the doctor is right, and the pill can somehow take care of your stomach ache, wouldn't you feel entitled to a little more time to discuss the problem?

That's exactly how most prospects feel when salespeople try to rush them through the interviewing stage (or, all too often, vault over it entirely).

Building on the rapport

Here's a sure-fire line for starting the interview process off right. You say,

---

Mr. Jones, would it help if I told you something about me and my company first?

Inevitably Mr. Jones will say "yes," allowing you to launch into a brief summary of your business. Keep it short, but cover the key areas. You might say, for example,

---

Mr. Jones, we've been in business for the last fifteen years. We've trained 250,000 people and we specialize in such areas as cold calling and prospect management. Let me give you an example . . .

. . . and you give a short example of a customer you've been able to help. Now, what do you accomplish by framing the initial question in this way? You involve Mr. Jones in the process. Even if the unlikely occurs, and Mr. Jones responds with something like,

---

No, I should tell you something about *us* first . . .

. . . the prospect is involved and the interview can proceed.

Here's an example based on an actual interview a DEI salesperson conducted with a recent prospect. As you read it, remember that the goal is to build on the rapport you've set up already, not to sound like an android reciting a list of prewritten queries.

You: Would it help if I told you a little bit about us first?

Prospect: Yeah.

You: Well, we started business in 1979. We've trained about 200,000 salespeople throughout the United States in a variety of business areas. Our firm has been able to help a lot of companies increase their sales effectiveness dramatically. (Pause.)

Prospect: Is that right. 200,000, huh?

You: 200,000. Now, at this point I'd like to ask you something if I may, Bob: did you ever have a sales trainer come and work with your company?

Prospect: No; you know, we've never had anybody come in here before on that level. I don't know, it's something we never really pursued before.

You: Okay. And what do you have right now? In terms of salespeople?

Prospect: Around the country, I'd say something like 500.

You: Wow; that's quite a staff. How do you keep track of them all?

Prospect: We're going to have quarterly meetings next year, and a big annual meeting in December.

You: Okay. Five hundred salespeople. That's kind of interesting. Now, what's the future? What are you trying to accomplish? What are your goals with this staff?

Prospect: Well, you know, we've been clobbered lately because of the competition, and we're really working on a couple of things right now to turn that around. Basically, we want to win back some of the market we lost last year, that's what it comes down to.

You: Okay. And how do you want to do that?

Prospect: We're bringing out a new line in August. . .

There are two main advantages to using this technique in a spontaneous, natural way.

Number one, of course, is that you're getting important information that will help you in the later stages of the sale.

Number two is almost as important: when done in a relaxed, non-confrontational style, this approach will help you demolish one of the worst stereotypes that will, whether you like it or not, tend to undermine your work as a salesperson: namely, that you want to ram some product or service down the prospect's throat whether or not he or she really needs it. Here's another example.

You: Andy, just out of curiosity—have you ever brought in a sales trainer before?

Prospect: Yeah, we did.

You: You did. Okay. How did it work out?

Prospect: Well, we really weren't happy with what they did. I'll tell you the truth, the guys came in here, issued orders for a couple of hours, then they left. We never saw them again. Didn't deliver any results to speak of, really.

You: Okay. That's good that you told me that; I'm going to talk to you in a little bit about our follow-up program that will prevent any problems like that. All right. Now, I'm just wondering, how many salespeople do you have right now?

Prospect: I've got 73 salespeople.

You: Are you happy with what they're doing?

Prospect: I could be happier.

You: Gotcha. What kind of training are they getting now?

Prospect: Not much. I mean, that's part of the problem. We're sort of trusting their ability to improvise, and I'm not crazy about that.

You: And you had a bad experience in the past.

Prospect: Yeah, absolutely.

You: Okay. And what are you planning for the future?

Prospect: Well, like I said, we have 73 salespeople right now. I'd like to get that up to 120 by August.

People will open up to you once you start asking questions—as long as you show some respect for what they're after, not what you're after.

Another technique that's extremely useful throughout the interview process is what we at DEI Management call "parable questioning." This technique uses stories and anecdotes to raise issues.

You know, Mr. Jones, I was working with a client the other day and they felt the color white was not really going to work in their operation. What do you think? Will it work here?

I met with a company recently, Ms. Smith, and they were really dissatisfied with their current suppliers. Does that describe you, too?

You know, it seems to me, after dealing with a lot of clients over the past 22 years, that this plan makes a lot of sense. What do you think?

Two things are accomplished when you frame your questions in this way. First, you have a chance to give examples of what you've done before, thereby establishing yourself as a person of experience. Second, you engage the client further in the process by inviting his or her opinion or inquiring into his or her needs.

Remember . . . by taking the trouble to ask these sorts of questions, you are automatically distinguishing yourself from the vast majority of salespeople—those who have their eye on ramming the product down the prospect's throat, without taking the slightest interest in a potential customer's needs.

When you ask about the past, present, and future, you're going to get a tremendous amount of information. And that's very good, because the more information you have, the more you're going to be able to customize your approach . . . and further distance yourself from the unflattering stereotypes that often surround salespeople.

Bearing all of that in mind, take a look at the next example. It's another interview that actually took place, and shows how you can pull someone in that "maybe/maybe not" group over to your side.

You: Bill, let me ask you a question.

Prospect: Sure.

You: Have you ever had a sales training program here before?

Prospect: Well, no, not really.

You: All right. Now when you say "not really," do you mean you've talked about it, or . . . ?

Prospect: We thought about it, but, you know, in the real estate business we just don't have time for it. That's more or less the way I feel at this point about sales training.

When you confront a bona-fide objection at this stage, don't overdo your response. Stay where you want to be—in the fact-gathering mode. At the very most, use one of the effective turnaround techniques we learned about in the prospecting stage, then keep going—tactfully. Be sure you're listening to what's been said.

You: Okay. I understand that. You know, a lot of the real estate people we're working with now told me exactly the same thing at first. Listen, just out of curiosity, how many people have you got selling here? How are you training them?

Prospect: Well, I've got about 54 reps right now, and, to tell you the truth, we're not training them.

You: Not at all?

Prospect: Nothing to speak of.

You: And how do you feel about their performance? (Pause.)

Prospect: Honestly?

You: Sure. Honestly. I can take it.
Prospect: (Laughs.) Well, to be frank, I've felt for a good month or so that we're not getting the kinds of results we want.

You: Okay. That was the feeling I got from you. Let me ask you, though: this is a new unit, right? What do you need to accomplish here?

> *Prospect:* Well, my goal with this unit is to sell about five million dollars worth of real estate in the next two months.

. . . and off you go. You're getting the information you need. Little by little, you begin to focus in on opportunities you have to help this prospect—who is different from your last prospect, and who will be different from your next prospect.

What's your cue to move on to the next stage—presentation? It's a low-level assent; a "this-could-be-interesting" kind of response. Remember, you're not talking about a sale yet; you're talking about permission to proceed to the next stage.

The low-level assent could be unspoken. Many salespeople report situations in which they simply "know the prospect is ready" to move on to the specifics of the product or service. On the other hand, the assent might be volunteered by the prospect, and could sound like one of the following:

> Well; where do we go from here?
>
> What's our next step?
>
> What can you tell me about the widget upgrade you mentioned earlier?

Obviously, some prospects will not offer such clear signposts, and won't be all that easy to "read", either. In these cases, the link to the next stage may be accomplished by asking something like this:

Well, what I'd like to do now, Mr. Prospect, is tell you a little bit about how I think the X-43 can help increase your production. How does that sound?

Bear in mind that your low-level assent may not come at all during the first interview. This brings us to the important topic of follow-up visits.

The follow-up

The end of the interview stage may or may not be the moment where you decide to conclude this meeting and set up another one—at which point, presumably, you would attempt to move on to the presentation stage, and perhaps even close the sale.

Depending on your product, your pricing, your competition, your level of knowledge, your instincts about the prospect's feeling toward your work so far, and any number of other factors, you may decide that the best course of action is something like this:

You: Mr. Jones, I'll tell you what I'd like to do. Let me go back to the office. Let me work up a couple of (quotes or programs or proposals) for you, and then I'd like to come back next Tuesday at three p.m. and give you some ideas, and I'll be able to show you in detail exactly how we can help you out.

I can't make the decision for you as to whether or not to try to close on the first meeting, but I would say that if you have any doubt about the matter whatsoever, it's probably a good idea to wait. But be sure to set the appointment then and there—don't take the hesitant and counterproductive step of promising to "call sometime later in the week and set things up." Set things up now. There is no better time.

"Etiquette"—and smooth communication with your office

As far as interviewing "etiquette" is concerned, the simplest rule is to present an appropriate professional image wherever possible. For instance, don't call your office only to be put on hold for ten minutes in front of your prospect. The message that's going to convey is that you don't count for much in the company—and, by extension, that the prospect doesn't count for much, either.

In that instance, you might decide to set up some sort of signal with your office when you're in this situation, so that you can either get a quick response or a discreet message that the information you need isn't available yet. It might be the word "stage"—since that's what you're on!

Say,

"Hi, Laurie, it's Carl. Listen, do you know what stage Leo is at in putting those production figures together for me?"

Don't say,

"Laurie, listen, it's Carl. I'm sitting right now with my prospect, Mr. Big. I need to talk to Leo about those production figures. Laurie, my prospect is a very important fellow, and, to be quite frank about it, he doesn't want me to waste time talking to you, or watching me sit here like an idiot listening to you explain what the problem is about getting through to Leo. So would you please just have Leo drop everything now and talk to me if it's at all possible?"

The rules the meeting will write for itself

The guidelines and dialogues that appear in this chapter will help you to move smoothly through the interviewing stage. However, you shouldn't rely on these "rules" too heavily.

The interview is, by definition, where you find out about the prospect's needs. If something unexpected takes place, and you're still communicating well and learning more about the prospect, don't sweat it too much.

If you develop the proper rapport, you'll be amazed at what can happen during the interview. It's simply not worthwhile to try to formulate a set of hard-and-fast rules about what is and isn't proper etiquette in an appointment.

Beyond the basics (like, oh, not carrying your dirty laundry around in your briefcase), it all depends on the chemistry you establish with the prospect. If things are really "clicking" between you, you may find a situation like this unfolding quite naturally:

Prospect: So when did you work with DEF company?

You: We did a project for them about six months ago. We had some fantastic results with that firm. If I remember correctly, they had a 25 percent sales increase after our program. Now that was over a two-week seminar; very intense.

Prospect: Wow. Twenty-five percent in two weeks. Now, that's not the three-day seminar we've been discussing.

You: No; that had a lot more in-depth, person-to-person work.

Prospect: That is quite a jump.

You: You know, I've got the correspondence on that project outside, you should see what that sales manager said about us in the letter they sent. Tell you what—let me go out to the car and get it. Stay right here, I'll be back in a flash. Do you mind?

Prospect: Not at all; go ahead.

Now, any rational person is going to be able to tell you that in most settings, it's hardly standard procedure to walk out of a meeting with the prospect to fish something out of the trunk of the car. But when the environment is right, something that extreme can seem completely natural.

How do I know? Because I had that very conversation with one of my prospects, and I closed the sale!

SUMMARY
Chapter Five:
Interviewing

✔ Remember that your goal in meeting with the client at all is to satisfy his or her needs with your product or service.

✔ Obtain information; provide information; inspire trust.

✔ Only 35 percent of our communication is verbal; the rest is non-verbal. Strive to make the non-verbal message you convey be, "I can help you."

✔ Look at the person with whom you'll be speaking.

✔ Adjust your speaking style to match the prospect's.

✔ Get a quick fix, if convenient and appropriate, on the sort of person you're dealing with. Remember Jung's four main communication styles: intuitors, thinkers, feelers, and sensors.

✔ Initially, provide a very brief summary of your company's success with other clients; then retreat from that subject, and make the prospect feel comfortable by isolating one element of the prospect's surroundings, hobbies, or work, and finding a way to make him or her feel a little bit better about discussing it.

✔ Avoid the trap of giving away too much information too soon.

✔ Be prepared for nothing to happen; keep your perspective, and realize that the sales cycle incorporates nineteen "no" answers for every "yes."

✔ Be prepared for anything to happen; once you "connect" with your prospect, opportunities are likely to present themselves.

✔ All selling is really listening.

✔ People buy things based on their emotions, and then try to find intellectually sound reasons to justify their intuition.

✔ There are three main areas of inquiry (past, present, and future) that you need to explore with a new prospect. Each of these three areas can be broken down further into a "what" and a "how" question.

✔ When you confront a bona fide objection during the interview stage, don't overdo your response. Address the concern and appeal to past success, but stay where you want to be—in the fact-gathering mode.

✔ A low-level assent will mark your transition into the next stage.

Chapter Six

Presentation or, The Outline

Verifying that you've got it right

Having noted all the concerns of the prospect through careful listening and note-taking during the interviewing stage, you're ready to move toward the presentation stage. There's just one crucial step to take first: the outline.

An outline? What am I talking about? Let me explain. The presentation has one basic purpose: to convince the prospect that your product or service answers the prospect's need, by which I mean, it fits what he or she *does*. In order to bring your prospect to that point of agreement, something crucial has to happen. You have to *verify* that your information is correct.

Too often, this step is left out of the sales process, with disastrous results. The salesperson makes a date with the prospect to come back (say, in a week) to make a presentation, fully believing that the prospect is "playing ball." In reality, the two parties aren't even close. Why? The salesperson has not verified the information. If the information in the presentation is wrong, the sale is not going to go through. It's as simple as that.

Let's look into this a little further. When someone doesn't buy from you, it's because the information you've presented is not "correct": it doesn't fit. Could be the price is wrong. Could be the client doesn't like you. Could be the product or service isn't right. Whatever the reason, it's absolutely essential that you find this out *before you attempt to close the sale*. If you don't, and the client decides not to buy, that's it: you probably won't get another chance.

So instead of going straight from the Interview to the Presentation, take the time to verify your information. Selling must include some verification of the information, even if this does not constitute a separate stage. Here's how it works. You ask the client if it's all right if you tell something about yourself; the client says "yes." You describe some of the things you do; then you ask the three basic questions: past, present, and future. In other words, you have a pretty good meeting. Then you say something like this:

Mr. Jones, here's what I'd like to do. I'd like to go back to my office and discuss what you and I have talked about with my manager [owner, president, mother, whatever]. Then, if it's all right with you, I'd like to to come back next week with an outline [proposal, treatment, whatever] and show you my thinking.

Note that key word "thinking."

Now, at this point, the client can either say "yes" or "no." If the answer is "yes," obviously you're going to set up your next appointment—and I mean set it up right then and there. (You want to move the sale along, right?) If the answer is "no," don't panic; the conversation isn't over. You simply say,

---

Mr. Jones, is there something that doesn't make sense here? What do I have to do differently?

You'll be surprised at how often this approach will yield important information and raises all the objections now rather than later.

Finally, when you have all the information you need, head back to your office and work through what you think you're going to present: the basic premise of the product or service and how it's going to fit what the prospect does. Write this information up in a one- or two-page proposal and bring it along to your next meeting.

Now you have something to work with. This is crucial! As you go over the outline with your prospect, several things will happen. You'll find out whether the prospect is serious, whether there is something to continue to talk about, and whether your information is correct. Most importantly, you will flush out every objection the prospect may be harboring about your product or service. What more nonthreatening environment could you ask for raising and meeting objections? If the prospect likes what you're doing, you're moving ahead. If the prospect doesn't like it, you're going to go back and change some things. Either way, you're still in the process. The important thing is this: you're finding out about any stumbling blocks now, before it's too late.

In some sales settings, of course, the outline will be less formal, and you may actually end up doing it "on your feet." Here's an example of how the transition out of the interview might look. It doesn't have to be anything fancy, and the presentation itself doesn't have to be longwinded, either.

You: Joan, can I ask if you've handled the acquisition of a new phone system before?

Prospect: I'm pretty new here; I just came on

a little over two months ago. So no, actually, I haven't.

You: All right. And are you people comfortable with the phone system you are currently using?

Prospect: Well, not really.

You: Okay. That's good to know. What would you like to see in your next system?

Prospect: Most of the complaints we have now center around the lines coming in. Customers often get busy signals, and the salespeople would like some of the features we've seen in ads for other systems.

You: Right. And I'm guessing those would be features like speed dialing, conference calling, or speakers, perhaps?

Prospect: Right. Those keep coming up in discussions, especially the conference calling.

After hearing some kind of low-level assent (which, of course, can come in as many different forms as there are prospects), it may be appropriate to move on to presentation:

Prospect: Now, do you folks offer that? What kind of system is it you're offering?

You: Well, let me give you an example. Our XYZ system can increase your incoming call capability, which would take care of those busy signals your customers get. And it has all those features we've mentioned here and is very easy to learn. The conference calling option can be very helpful in boosting your productivity, as you might imagine.

Joan, let me tell you a little about the kinds of companies we typically are able to help. Widgets Unlimited, which I believe is in your business, just signed on with an XYZ system. I was over there yesterday, and they just love the system. Now, we determined that, for a company of that size. . .

And on it goes. Obviously, the specific information about your product or service can only be supplied by you.

Of course, in some settings, and with some products or services, the presentation will be a little more detailed and extensive, perhaps something like this:

You: Well, John, having heard what you've told me about your organization, let me make a suggestion to you. We've just finished a program in which we were able to increase the overall effectiveness of the ABC Widget Company's sales staff by 12 percent. What we did was, after taking a look at the people, we decided that the best approach would be a multi-session program that would offer three three-hour sessions over a period of two weeks.

> The idea would be that this program would comprise about nine hours of training in all. That's the kind of setting in which we've really been able to deliver results.

Remember, you're not ready to close yet—you want to see the reaction to this idea. So after having outlined this, move on to more general territory.

> Now let me show you something else, too. This is our client list. One of the things we believe in, and that we've emphasized with virtually all these companies, is the importance of prospecting as the basis of the sales cycle. .

At this point, you might talk about those elements of the product or service you feel are of greatest interest to the prospect.

Reacting to signals

In the next dialogue, look how the presentation stage changes when the information you receive is a little bit different—say, by learning that the prospect feels strongly about the virtues of holding one-day programs (rather than two-week programs) for time reasons.

Notice, too, that the structure is fluid—if the prospect seems to require a slightly different approach, that's no problem at all.

> *You:* Now, I understand your time con-

straints, Mary, because I remember your mentioning to me earlier the importance of trying to pull the whole program together in one day. So let me show you what I would do. I would take this day, divide it into three segments, and do prospecting, prospect management, and selling skills, all in one clip. That's a pretty full day for them—but, you know, I can tell you from experience that it will work if we manage it right. What I like to do is follow up a little bit later—and the timing is certainly wide open—follow up with the program on sales management, which consolidates things and can do a lot to ensure their success.

You see, there are two things that we really believe in strongly, Mary. Number one is the importance of periodic professional development for salespeople—that's one of the things, in our experience anyway, that really distinguishes the winners from the losers, and can help you battle high burnout and turnover rates. And number two is the crucial role that prospecting plays in the sales cycle. . .

The seven commandments

Of the four stages, I've found that it's in presentations that salespeople can customize their approach most easily. As we've seen, some products or services might require in-depth reviews of the product history and typical applications; others won't take quite so long to execute effectively.

Nevertheless, some common standards exist. Over the years, I've found that there are seven basic rules that apply to this stage of the sale. If you break one of these rules, it's a pretty decent bet that you'll lose the sale. It's that simple. Whatever you do with the sales dialogues that follow in this section, be absolutely sure that you abide by the Seven Commandments of Presentation.

The Seven Commandments of Presentation

I. Thou shalt listen before all else.

II. Thou shalt maintain eye contact.

III. Thou shalt not misquote the prospect in order to advance the cycle.

IV. Thou shalt never argue with the client to prove thy points, for even winning such a dispute, thou shalt in reality lose.

V. Thou shalt never interrupt the prospect.

VI. Thou shalt offer constant proof of thy claims, preferably with the names of thy current satisfied customers.

VII. Thou shalt strive, not to close the sale, but first and foremost to help thy prospect, and to allow him or her to feel that your visit has been a profitable one.

The transition, revisited

Here's another good example of the entry into the presentation stage.

You: John, have you ever bought life insurance before?

Prospect: No. My employers have always provided me with sufficient coverage—but I've been thinking about adding a little more now that I have a couple of kids.

You: Fine. So mostly through the companies you've worked for up to this point.

Prospect: Exactly.

You: And how much coverage do you currently have?

Prospect: I'm carrying $100,000 now.

You: Okay. So, I can see how you'd want to extend that with a family now. And how much had you been thinking about increasing that to, roughly?

Prospect: I'd been considering doubling that.

You: Doubling it. Okay. You know, John, our policy will easily give you what you're looking for. And I do have a plan you may be interested in looking at that can provide some important benefits for your spouse, too.

After you've described how you'd like to help the prospect, continue with a more general description of your firm's goals or your special approaches to your customers as a whole.

One of the things we try hardest to do, John, is provide you with a real broad range of options. For instance. . .

Pride goeth before a fall

One problem I've encountered in my presentation work with salespeople is the tendency to read too much into an interview stage that's gone well.

You may know the cycle yourself. You ask the client about what his or her needs are, and you get such positive feedback that you think to yourself, "Hey! I've got this one cinched!"

So you do something very dangerous. You take the prospect for granted.

It's nothing that uncommon; most salespeople lose a few this way at first. If I've swapped life stories with my prospect, gotten him to talk about himself, and piqued his interest about my company, what am I supposed to do? Feel terrible?

Not at all. But the fact that I as a salesperson may think I'm pretty hot stuff right about now is completely irrelevant. The point is to make sure that the prospect knows he's done the right thing in making a decision to buy. That's how I make my money, and that's how you make your money.

Whatever notches get placed on your ego during the sale are not the prospect's concern. Remember, it's from the prospect's point of view that you must close the sale; and the prospect's only relevant concern at this point is whether the product or service will solve a given problem.

"Yeah, but what do I say?"

Because the presentation stage is probably the most

open-ended of the four stages, actually putting together the words that constitute your presentation can be a little bewildering for some salespeople. Let's face it: no one "pitch" is going to be right for all salespeople in all industries. Here's the best advice I can give you on determining your game plan for this stage.

Remember our old friends features, benefits, and proof? All three usually make an appearance of some sort during this stage.

The potential benefit should be fairly clear to your prospect by now, as you've highlighted it throughout the earlier stages. It's the whole reason for your visit. Certainly, though, you should take every opportunity to reinforce the potential benefit of your product or service, even if the main outline is fairly clear at this stage.

Features are of interest, too, but to a much lesser degree than either of the other two factors. The fact that a pair of green rubber boots has new vulcanized high-stress supertough linings is good to know, but not as important as knowing what boots will actually do for you (keep your feet dry) or who else uses them (40 percent of the population of Seattle, one of the rainiest cities in the country).

The fact is, at this stage, it is probably the proof that is most important to your sales efforts. You should be certain to reassure your prospect with ample helpings of company names and/or personal contacts who've sworn by your product or service.

A friendly reminder

Let me repeat that note of caution regarding "people proof," which can play such a crucial role during the presentation stage.

It's a very bad idea to circulate the names of every professional contact you know without clearing this sort of use. A tactful mention to your existing clients that you'd like to be able to mention their name and company to prospective customers usually does the trick. It will be extremely rare for someone to deny you this kind of permission (after all, "networking" is at the heart of most professional career success), but when there is a problem, you should know about it and respect the wishes of your customer.

Success stories

Where appropriate, then, add proof and real-life examples throughout your in-person meeting—but be especially vigilant about it here at the presentation stage. It is always to your advantage to point out who else in the prospect's field has been bowled over by your firm's quality and/or results.

This is especially important if you are selling a service that your prospect is likely to consider an "intangible" item. You must make it real, valid, concrete—it has to become much less abstract in his or her mind. If you're selling financial services, for instance, you must continually endorse your product with real examples of actual dollar performance for real people. You have to be able to tell the prospect something like this:

You: You know, Mrs. Letitia Jones, out in West Covina, California, had kept her money in a peanut butter jar for 46 years. Once she decided to invest with us, she was able to see a return of fourteen and a half billion dollars in one month. Let me show you what we did for her.

Or (assuming you haven't cleared such activities with Letitia):

You: Now this is an interesting plan. You know, a lovely old lady out in West Covina, California, 92 years old, made fourteen and a half billion dollars with this plan. One month. Pretty amazing, huh? Let me show you what we did for her.

Well, credibility counts for something too. Maybe you don't want an example quite that impressive. But you get the idea.

The fact is, nobody wants to be anyone's first customer. People want to see how it's worked before. Who's done well with it. Where the results are. At this stage, people want something tangible, something they can trust. So that's going to be one of your goals: To provide them with proof at some point during your presentation.

Making progress

It goes without saying that during your presentation (indeed, at any given moment in the sale), you have to be prepared for the prospect to progress to the next stage. After all, the objective of each stage is to get to the next one, right?

We're usually so eager to handle the objections that can materialize at any given moment, we forget to keep our eyes open for opportunity. It does work the other way, as well—prospects can find themselves more and more interested in your product, and less and less interested in hearing you talk about it. If that's the case, you might consider shortening your presentation and moving on to the close.By the same token, not all sales will close with the first meeting. More than one visit may well be required—depending on signals you get from the prospect. Only you can judge whether or not another appointment is appropriate. Keep your eyes open to the prospect's reactions, and act accordingly. If you're in any doubt, it's probably not a good sign.

How to deliver a losing presentation

How do sales get lost? A lot of the time they're lost on presentations that finish up like this:

Prospect: Gee, this all looks very interesting. But you know what, I'd have to clear it with my boss.

You: Oh. I thought this was a decision that you. . .

Prospect: No, no, I'd have to bring her in on it.

You: Okay. Well, ah, when should I come back?

It should come as no surprise to you now that sentences like "When should I come back?" are momentum-killers. They take you out of the driver's seat.

Who knows when is good? You'll probably be asked to call later to confirm an appointment "sometime next week," which, all too often, means never. And who's to say, for that matter, what the prospect will or won't say to the boss?

It's a decent bet that nothing at all will happen—not out of any dislike for you or your product, but simply because of the crisis-oriented nature of so much of modern business. If you're there, you're a priority. If you're not. . .

It's really a question of attitude, and this all-important issue is essential when it comes to any discussion of the presentation stage.

Remember: your goal in any stage of the sales cycle is to move to the next stage, not to stall out right where you are. In the example above, your instincts should be honed to such a high degree that "When should I come back?" isn't offered as a response at all.

Of course, there's a fine line between pushy, manipulative selling and good, old-fashioned aggressive selling. It's a line, however, that most good salespeople can identify.

So let's go back to our example. What should you do when the prospect interrupts you in mid-sentence and says,

---

Prospect: . . .I'd have to clear it with my boss.

We've addressed similar problems by using a straightforward attempt to reschedule: "Is Tuesday at three okay?" I suggest an equally straightforward comeback here.

You: Hey, I understand. Tell you what. Let's go do it now. Where's her office?

No waffling. No discontented looks. No staring at your shoes. Upbeat, positive, and enthusiastic. Now, it is certainly possible that you're going to have to reschedule anyway. I'm not saying that using this approach will solve the problem automatically. But I am saying that it's much more likely to get you positive feedback than the first dialogue I outlined.

For that matter, this optimistic, enthusiastic approach is exactly what you should bring to the entire presentation stage.

Of datebooks and calendars

While we're on the subject of revisiting the prospect, let me add a word of warning: carry your datebook with you so you can set your second or follow-up appointment.

A note is probably also in order on the kinds of datebooks available. Please, please, please stay away from those card-a-day, pocket systems that display your life story and your appointments for the next month and a half.

Why? Well, we've learned that 65 percent of all that is communicated to the prospect is nonverbal, right? What's the nonverbal message you're conveying when you open up such a book in front of a prospect?

"Look at all my other customers! I'm so busy, I can hardly keep track of all the business! Why, if I were to lose your little card, it would be just as if you'd dropped off the face of the earth!"

All the prospect cares about is when you're coming back. To pass along the message that the prospect is just one of many, many others is a big mistake.

Slow: closing stage ahead

That's the main structure of the presentation stage. Next, we're going to talk about closing—though you should bear in mind that the actual closing process is by no means an automatic development.

Before barreling into the sale's final stages, you need to take the time to listen to the prospect. You need to find out his or her reaction to what you've laid out in your presentation. How does he or she feel about what you've outlined? Good? Bad? Indifferent?

I've come up with a revolutionary way of obtaining

that information after your initial presentation.

Here's what it looks like:

You: So, Mr. Prospect: how does what I've just outlined sound to you?

The moment of truth

If the prospect says, "Hey, it sounds great. It's just what we're looking for," then you've entered the closing process. If the prospect says, "Gee, I don't know, I'm worried about such-and-such," then you're still in the presentation stage. Complicated, huh?

(Of course, the end of your first presentation attempt is definitely a point at which you can expect to face some objections. Once again, the important subject of handling these situations will be covered in detail later on in the book.)

In the next chapter, we'll get the rest of the story on how to close sales effectively.

SUMMARY
Chapter Six:
Presentation

✔ The structure of the presentation stage should be fluid, and should allow for a good deal of customization on your part.

✔ Follow the Seven Commandments.

✔ Don't read too much into an interview stage that's gone well. If you become overconfident during the presentation stage, you stand a good chance of losing the sale.

✔ Features, benefit, and proof should be part of your presentation. Special emphasis on proof, particularly "people proof," is often required.

✔ Nobody wants to be someone's first customer. Where appropriate, then, provide real-life examples throughout your presentation—but be careful not to circulate too freely the names of professional contacts without clearing this sort of use.

✔ Be prepared to move on to the next stage; follow the prospect's lead.

✔ Avoid momentum-killing phrases like, "When should I come back?"

✔ Stay upbeat, positive, and enthusiastic; this attitude is much more likely than any other to result in positive feedback from the prospect.

✔ When the groundwork has been properly laid, attempt to initiate the transition into the closing stage by asking the prospect how he or she feels about what you've outlined.

Chapter Seven

Closing

No guarantees

Let me remind you, before we go any further, that sales is an extremely unpredictable way to make a living.

You probably know that already, but I remind you of it here in order to supply some perspective on the task of closing. That perspective is crucial, and it ties into the act of putting together any section of a book and saying that it's going to tell you how to "close the sale."

"Verifying" the sale

If I had my way, I'd refer to this stage as "verifying" the sale, rather than "closing" it. When it's done correctly, the final stage of an in-person meeting, far from closing anything, opens doors. It's a mutual decision to do business together.

Nevertheless, in the world in which we live, personality, trust, and individual persuasiveness play huge roles in determining peoples' levels of success. And the fact is, you just can't depend on the prospect to take the initiative to get things moving.

As we learned much earlier on, your success depends, in large measure, on a straightforward willingness to ASK for the sale—and since this process is the final stage in your prospect's transition from "lead" to customer, it makes a certain amount of sense to consider it the close of something.

The technique we'll be discussing, as you may remember, is called "assumptive closing." It allows you to focus in on the details of a given sale, rather than asking the prospect's permission to grant the sale in the first place.

I'm addressing it at this point in the book because, after dutifully working with you through the first three stages, some of your prospects will in fact be ready to sign on with you at this point. Others will not. You probably won't know ahead of time.

Those who don't say "yes" will probably deliver up an objection or two. We'll address this possibility, as well.

Right now, we'll be talking about the actual mechanics of closing the sale, and dealing with the challenges and opportunities that accompany this stage. You may be surprised to learn that, if you've followed the previous steps, it's a lot simpler than you think.

Winners and losers

Because the closing stage is usually the one a salesperson is most likely to "do anything" to see through successfully, I'd like to take a moment to talk about how we look at sales as a profession, and the ethics that surround it.

I hope it's clear by this point in the book that I view the entire sales cycle as a partnership, a mutual progression of salesperson and prospective customer through distinct stages. It should be self-evident, then, that no one stage can stand independently of any other—least of all the final one.

Many overaggressive salespeople, however, take an approach to their work that bypasses the needs of the prospect and makes a mockery of the idea of working through the cycle at all. If they can just get the sales in today, these reps seem to think, the rest of the stuff will take care of itself . . . and if the customer isn't completely satisfied, or is presented with circumstances other than those he was led to expect, well, there are other fish in the sea. Some sales-people even deliberately mislead the prospect or distort the record or performance ability of their products.

When salespeople adopt this mindset, they leave out the most crucial element of a successful sales career—the insistence on filling the needs of the customer. Once you take out that ingredient, you're using someone else's system, not mine.

Nothing that appears in this book (and certainly nothing in this section on closing) will be of any use to you if you forget the customer.

I'll say it again. If you ignore the customer, my system simply won't do you any good. Everything I'm suggesting is predicated on the idea that you will develop an intimate understanding of the prospect's problems and business needs, and that a certain amount of legitimately-placed trust has grown between you . . . trust that you are committed to *proving* well-placed.

If you don't build up that trust (or, worse still, build it up through dishonest means), not only will you have difficulty building up a client base, but you'll also burn out, ultimately finding sales to be an unrewarding profession.

Two good reasons to put the customer first

Let's take a look at each of those outcomes separately.

Why will you have difficulty building up a client base? Because repeat sales are the life-blood of the bigger commission checks. If you consistently mislead or lie to your prospects, it goes without saying that you're not going to have a lot of people knocking on your door asking for more. Quite to the contrary, you're going to have a lot of angry former customers walking around saying nasty things about you. Negative commercials, if you will.

Why will you burn out more quickly? Because you'll only be "winning" in the short term (that is to say, that day's sales). After a while, you'll lose your initiative. You'll realize that you're on the lookout for people to exploit, not people to help. Most people (not all, but most) find it extremely difficult to motivate themselves over the long haul for that kind of work. You won't have built up the long-term relationships with associates that make for real career satisfaction. You'll become isolated; it will be tougher for you to do the prospecting work every day; you won't look forward to meeting new prospects. Why should you? Two months from now, they're not going to want to hear your name.

We've come across the fundamental paradox that accompanies a career in sales. "Winners" in sales win by taking the interests and needs of others—their prospects and clients—to heart and setting their objectives accordingly. "Losers" stunt their own career growth and short-circuit their financial objectives when they lose sight of the customer's requirements.

In a fundamental sense, "closing the sale," independent of the wishes or needs of your prospect, is an impossible task. Completing the sale, affirming the work you've done, beginning a partnership—these are attainable goals. But they require that you work with your potential customer. That doesn't mean you can't use "aggressive" techniques in the final stages—as we'll see, I'm recommending that you be quite forthright in your vision of how the partnership is to proceed. But you cannot work in a vacuum.

Without contented customers, a salesperson is an irrelevancy.

The assumptive close

During my seminars, I usually address the topic of closing the sale sometime on the second or third day with a group. Here's what I say.

> Good morning. Today we're going to talk
> about closing skills for you people—the na-
> tional sales force of ABC, Incorporated. Now,
> the first thing I want to do is for everyone to
> take out their wallet or purse and place in on
> the desk, right in front of you. Okay? Let's go.

The group dutifully places the objects in full view.

> Okay. Great. Now what I'd like you to do is to
> open up your wallet or purse and take out a
> one dollar bill.

Wallets and purses snap open, and a sea of dollar bills
materializes.

> Super. Now what I'm going to do is walk down
> the aisle here, and I'm going to collect those
> dollar bills. Everybody please pass 'em to the
> center.
>   Okay? Here we go.

I move briskly down the aisle, collecting cash. Every
once in a while there's a shouted comment ("Is a twenty
okay?") or a laugh from the back of the room, but I pay no
mind. I continue collecting the money.

After I've collected everything, I take out my wallet,
place the bulging stack of bills in it, and say:

Thanks. The first lesson this morning is that
the single most effective way to get a sale,
once you've laid the groundwork, is to ASK.
    Any questions?

That demonstration has never failed.

(And, by the way, for the skeptics out there, this does work with the larger denominations, as well. I once tried asking for fifties, but the only person who had one was the company president, who happened to be sitting in on the seminar. He handed it over happily.)

Why does it work? Forget, for the moment, the fact that I always give the cash back—after a pause just long enough to make things interesting.

Notice that I said at the outset that I use this demonstration on the second day or later. Do you think that makes a difference?

Of course it does. If I walk in at nine o'clock in the morning on the first day and try to pull that stunt, what's going to happen? A lot of silence and no dollar bills, that's what. Maybe a few wary questions like, "What do you want the money for?" But that's about it.

My point should be clear. Once you've developed the necessary trust, once you've solidified yourself as a partner in the process, once you've taken the time to listen, the possibilities are endless. At nine a.m. on Day 1, I'm this guy the company says they're supposed to listen to. At nine a.m. on Day 2, I've asked them questions, supplied them with prospecting techniques, played them some tapes of actual sales, done roleplaying exercises . . . in short, I've made myself known to the group as someone who has their effectiveness and performance in mind. They know they can trust me. They know that if I ask them to pass a dollar bill to the center of the room, there's probably a good reason for it.

And there is! Believe me, thousands of salespeople have taken that demonstration to heart and improved their closing ratios dramatically. You can too.

Getting to the heart of the matter

When it comes to closing, salespeople tend to beat around the bush a great deal. That's tough for me to watch, because I hate to see sales get blown—probably almost as much as you do.

"How do I close a sale?" Hundreds of thousands of salespeople agonize over that question throughout their careers.

Why? It's not a tough question, really. We can answer that one. We know how to close a sale. We make the assumption that the sale will close. We ask for the sale in terms the prospect will find unthreatening. We try to initiate the paperwork. It's that simple.

Will we get shot down? Sometimes. But what other options are there? Continuing to babble away about how wonderful our widgets are? The prospect has heard it already! Ask for the sale. Then be quiet and see what kind of response you get.

Askaphobia

I've come up with a name for the disease that seems to make sure salespeople are too terrified to come right out and ask for the sale (the most effective closing method by far). I call the disease askaphobia. Its primary symptom is running off at the mouth during the close.

Askaphobia—the fear of asking—eats away at the entrails of far too many commission checks. Don't let it nibble into yours.

If you've worked through all the steps with your prospect, the most effective way to bring the visit to a successful conclusion is to use the "assumptive close." In other words, you will focus on a detail connected with the sale, and ask about that, assuming that the sale will close. And it should!

Here's another seemingly paradoxical point: my work indicates that it's vitally important that YOU believe the sale will close, and work from there. Most salespeople worry themselves sick about what the prospect thinks—and all too often, the prospect picks up that lack of confidence and makes a "no" decision on the spot!

Once you accept that you've done all the work necessary to find out whether the person is a valid prospect, to learn about his or her needs, and to present your product, you can accept that you should in fact close the sale, and proceed confidently from that point.

The fact is, if the proper groundwork has been laid, and if the prospect feels that the benefits of the product or service are genuine, and that the relevant concerns have been met, closing the sale is quite simple.

It might sound like this.

You: Well. How does what I've told you about our widgets sound so far?

Prospect: It sounds pretty good, Maureen.

You: Okay. That's great to hear. So, Mr. Prospect, you know what I'd like to do? I'd like to get that paperwork started now so that we can be in business next week. Was an April 1st delivery what you had in mind?

Note the way this is phrased. The focus is not on whether or not Mr. Prospect will please give us a sale; it's on a detail related to the product or service (in this case, the delivery date).

If the subsequent response is something other than an "it-sounds-pretty-good" type response, you are being told that there's a problem somewhere.

Don't get defensive; try to determine what the difficulty is. After hearing your prospect out, you may want to offer to work up a new proposal, and attempt to schedule a new appointment.

If you do decide to continue on this visit, do so with caution. Remember, you are back at the previous stage, presentation (or perhaps even interviewing). The prospect has told you openly that it's not appropriate to progress to the closing stage. Be absolutely sure you've addressed all the relevant concerns before attempting to close. For more ideas on this subject, see the next chapter.

Here are some variations on the "assumptive close."

You: So, Mr. Powers, how does what I've been discussing with you today about our telephone system sound?

Prospect: It sounds very interesting, Jane; very interesting.

You: That's great. Well, based on what we've done here today, here's what I can recommend to you. We can set you up with the Hercotron system at that special price I mentioned, and we can do it with eight phone lines out to your sales office. Was that what you had in mind?

You: And I guess what I'd like to ask now, Ms. Johnson, is what you think of what I've told you so far about the Zippomatic computer system?

Prospect: Well, I think it might have an application. It's certainly got a long list of features.

You: Absolutely. Well, I thought you'd be impressed with it, frankly, because a lot of other people in your field have reacted very positively. Okay; that's great. So my suggestion at this point would be for us to get the wheels turning, and to set up the software customization so we can get the system up and running to your specifications. Now would you be interested primarily in the accounting applications?

An approach that's this straightforward can be a little scary for some salespeople at first. That's natural. It may take a little time for you to adjust to so direct a technique. But I'm still going to suggest very strongly that you try it, for one simple reason. It's the most effective close I've ever come across.

Of course, it doesn't take an Einstein to figure out that some prospects won't immediately reject such a suggestion at this point, but won't be ready to make out a purchase order, either.

A typical response to this type of close will sound something like this:

Prospect: Hold it, hold it; back up. Now, April 1st is fine, but I'm not ready to make a decision on this yet. We haven't talked about the service plan.

That kind of a reaction is exactly what you want to hear!

After all, this is the first you've heard about a desire for a service plan! Polite, professional, firm "assumptive closing" is your best route to a "yes" if the prospect is ready, or more important information if the prospect is not.

Objections during the close—and how you can respond

We'll cover the topic of dealing with objections in exhaustive detail in the next chapter. However, there are four tried-and-true responses that are of particular interest during the closing stage. We'll look at each of them here.

As you might expect, the prospect's answer to the first "can-we-get-started" attempt will determine our next move in the close.

The downscale model response

If the application of the product and its usefulness seem firmly established in your prospect's mind, but he or she is wary about placing an initial order because of quantity or cost concerns, you may want to consider using the Downscale Model Response.

You: I can certainly understand your hesitation on the A-98, Mr. Jones; seven million dollars is a lot of money. But you know, a lot of our clients felt just the same way at first, before they learned about the A-99, which delivers superior performance at a very competitive price.

The future response

If you feel you've worked all your points into a convincing package for the prospect, but are having difficulty making the matter seem tangible, try the Future Response. It's one of the best ways to lend a healthy sense of reality to the sales visit.

You: Mr. Jones, one of the reasons I'd wanted to try to wrap this up is so we could lock in your rate; it seems like every month or so that the accounting people raise the prices on us, and I felt sure you'd want to avoid that. Now, we can guarantee this price for you; would you want me to go ahead and process the order on that basis?

The incentive response

Trying to pry an important customer from the competition? Looking for a way to get a large order off the ground for the first time? Consider the Incentive Response.

You: Well, as you know, Mr. Jones, I firmly believe that you're going to find that our widgets make your operation more productive and more profitable. So here's what I can do to get you started so we can prove that to you. Why don't we think about giving you a

free service contract on your widgets for the
first year?

(Note: If your sales manager has a problem with ma-
neuvers like these, you may face a roadblock. Clear everything ahead of time and you'll come out ahead.)

The endorsement response

One of the most popular closing responses is to return, in a dramatic way, to your people proof—which
should, of course, have been prominently displayed during
the presentation stage.

You: Mr. Jones, as I'd mentioned earlier, By-
ron Jordan over at 1234 Incorporated is
very happy with the A-99. Maybe we could
set up a conference call that would give you
the chance to talk with him about his percep-
tions of the product. What do you think?

Ask

What it boils down to in the end is a very simple rule.
Once you're certain that you've laid all the proper ground
work, you can feel confident in simply asking for the sale or
for more information that will help you reach the sale. Each
of the responses above makes use of that principle.

In making Power Sales Presentations, there's no
room for passive selling. Only active salespeople can make
things happen. I admit that the formula I'm suggesting to
you may be a little tough at first; accordingly, I strongly ad-
vise that you engage in some fairly extensive role-playing
centered on the idea of asking for the sale. A fellow sales-

person or a family member is usually a good candidate for such an exercise.

(Of course, role-playing is a recommended procedure for your work in all four stages; however, ignoring it while developing your closing techniques is particularly dangerous.)

Partnership

Remember, the goal is not to defeat the prospect; it's to build on the extensive work you've already done, and initiate a partnership. Keep the tone professional and non-threatening.

Maintain a firm, persistent approach. And never lose sight of the prospect's goals. If you can phrase your product in those terms closest to the prospect's objectives, my bet is that, more often than not, you'll find that your contact is simply looking for an opportunity to let you help solve problems.

SUMMARY
Chapter Seven:
Closing

✔ When it's done correctly, the final stage of an in-person meeting, far from closing anything, opens doors.

✔ Without contented customers, a salesperson is an irrelevancy.

✔ Once you've done the preliminary work correctly, the single most effective way to get a sale is to ASK.

✔ "Askaphobia" keeps many salespeople from performing up to their full potential. It's primary symptom is aimless talk during the closing stage.

✔ "Assumptive closing" focuses not on whether or not

the prospect will grant your wish and authorize a sale, but rather on a detail related to the product or service.

✔ Polite, professional assumptive closing is your best route to a "yes" if the prospect is ready, or more important information if the prospect is not.

✔ Specific techniques for dealing with objections during the closing stage include: the downscale model response; the future response; the incentive response; and the endorsement response.

✔ The goal is not to defeat the prospect, but to build on the extensive work you've done together, and initiate a partnership of sorts.

✔ Never lose sight of what the prospect wants.

Chapter Eight

Objections

Effective turnarounds

In this section, we're going to concentrate on the most effective methods you can use to turn around an objection.

This topic gets a separate part of the book for a simple reason: there's no one point in the sales cycle at which the prospect can be depended upon to present every one of his or her objections. It can happen anywhere, at any time, without warning.

In the earlier chapter on qualifying, we talked a little bit about one of the most effective basic turnaround techniques. But as I'm sure you know if you've been selling for any time at all, objections have a nasty habit of popping up throughout the cycle. Now it's time to look at how to handle them when they show up during the in-person interview.

During my seminars, I ask the participants to name the most common objections they encounter in their sales work. Two fascinating things that tend to happen.

The first is that there are some objections that come up again and again, no matter what the industry or the sales staff. The second is that, where there are industry-specific objections, the salespeople in that industry don't realize how often they themselves hear the same thing from the prospects, time after time!

Objections: the six basic types

Every objection can be broken down into one of six basic types: Stall, Hidden, Reassurance, Doubt, Hard, and Easy.

My bet is that, within those six types, there are specific objections associated with your firm's product or service for which you can be more prepared than you are. If you get anything out of this chapter, it is that, once you hear objection "X" for the fiftieth time, you should be more prepared to deal with it, and have a better idea of what works and what doesn't, than you did the first time you heard it.

Salesperson, heal thyself

It may seem unbelievable, but there are a great many salespeople who say to me, "Steve, they're telling me the product costs too much, what do I do?" And I say to them, "Well, have you ever heard that before?" And they say, "Hmm. . . come to think of it, yeah." And I say, "What did you say last time?" Then they say, "Well, that particular time, I told the prospect that we could deliver X, Y, and Z, and that if you looked at it in such-and-such a way, over the long run it really came out costing less." And I ask, "Did it work?" They say, "As a matter of fact, yeah, it did."

Then I say, "Why don't you try that, then?" And they say, "Great, thanks a lot!"

Sometimes it's a tough life, being a sales trainer.

Let's go back for a moment to our great undiscovered salesperson, Bill Wambsgnass. How do you think he reacted, as a little child, the first time his mother or father threw a ball his way?

Like most of us would have as children, he probably just ducked, hoping to protect himself. My bet is that it wasn't until the third, fourth, or fifth time that he finally realized they were throwing the ball to him, not at him, and attempted to catch the ball.

Maybe after his first few attempts at trying to catch the ball, he learned that by putting his arms up in a certain position, he could knock the ball down in front of him. And perhaps from there he learned that, with a little more practice, he could actually catch it and throw it back.

That's exactly the progression most salespeople go through when they begin trying to manage objections. Most of them, in the early stages, simply duck for cover, trying to protect themselves. They don't try to "catch" the objection, meet it, and return the dialogue to the prospect. They assume the prospect is trying to knock them down, attack them somehow, and the exchanges quickly become polarized as unnecessary conflicts arise. That, obviously, is not the environment in which you want to do business.

Too many salespeople are taken by surprise when it comes to objections. Too many salespeople think the prospect is trying to pick a fight—rather than find a solution to a problem. Too many salespeople fail to see the objection for what it is—an opportunity.

What's really being said?

It is probably more important to understand where an objection comes from than the actual words used to express it. Words, by themselves, often don't give you all the information you need. In an objection (as in any other communication) the context is all-important. If I were to say to you, at the top of my voice, "Sit down," emphasizing the word "sit," you would know very quickly that I was angry. If, on the other hand, you'd just walked into my office, and I said to you, "Sit down," in a rather low tone, pointing to a chair, you'd know that I meant for you to sit down and relax.

Similarly wide variations in meaning accompany most of the standard objections. There's nothing I'd like more to be able to tell you than, "When they say this, it always means thus-and-so, and it always comes at this point in the presentation, and here's how you turn it around." But sales is a little more subtle than that.

Bill Wambsgnass tried-and-true three-step turnaround technique

Fortunately, there is an approach you can take that's proved very effective for many, many salespeople. It's a three-step system that helps you work with the prospects you encounter, not against them.

You don't have to incorporate this technique into your daily work, but I should warn you: our friend Bill Wambsgnass would have almost certainly practiced it until it was second nature.

The first step is to identify the objection. The second is to validate it. The third is to solve it.

Easier said than done.

The first step: identifying the objection

Your mental attitude—how you handle the split-second following the prospect's objection—is probably the single most important factor in determining your success in dealing effectively with the prospect's concerns. What happens in that split-second will determine whether you know what you're up against.

When you hear an objection, your first mental reaction should be to identify it. Not to get defensive or to argue about whether or not the prospect is "right." Who cares about "right"? You want to be able to work with someone, not win arguments.

The six kinds of objections: a summary

In the following boxes, I've broken down the six main groups of objections. Reviewing the categories thoroughly will probably add quite a bit to your confidence level.

THE STALL, in which the prospect tries to "limbo-ize" your efforts by postponing any decision—usually permanently.

THE HIDDEN OBJECTION, in which the prospect is saying one thing but acting on a set of circumstances that's quite different.

THE HARD ONE, in which you run into a legitimate brick wall, and the prospect has a good reason to believe your product or service is unnecessary, inappropriate, too expensive, or a combination of all three.

THE EASY ONE, in which the prospect shows evidence of genuine interest in your product or service, but offers up a technicality that stands in the way—usually one you can overcome without much difficulty.

THE REASSURANCE REQUEST, in which your prospect has trouble accepting the consequences of making a decision, accepting risk, and/or exercising authority.

THE DOUBT AND FEAR RESPONSE, in which

an otherwise interested prospect develops a case of the willies—typically at the last minute.

Context is everything

Of course, such labels are useful only up to a point. As I've pointed out, you can get the exact same words coming out of someone's mouth in two different sales situations, but the meaning can be utterly different.

If you're at the very early stages of the sale, prospecting, let's say, and the person on the other end of the line says, "Gee, let me stop you, we have no interest whatsoever in that," then you're getting one message. The person is under the impression that your product or service isn't useful.

But if you're heading toward the close during your third visit with someone, having gone through extensive prospecting, interviewing, and presentation sessions, and your prospect suddenly turns to you and says, "Gee, let me stop you, we have no interest whatsoever in that," then something very different has happened. Specifically, something is seriously wrong with your interviewing skills. Either that, or you've got a prospect who's not being honest with you. (In that case, it's a good bet you're dealing with a problem that has not been resolved yet from the prospect's point of view.)

The second step: validating the objection

The second step is to validate the objection. In essence, this is done by repeating the prospect's objection back to him or her. Some salespeople find this quite difficult—they may feel that repeating the objection will solidify it in the prospect's mind, or that it will show that the salesperson is "wrong."

Baloney.

The objection is your prospect's reality. It is all you have to work with. It's already been solidified in the prospect's mind, otherwise the prospect wouldn't have said it in the first place. Your only alternative is to show the prospect you're listening by feeding the information back again. I can't emphasize the point too much: don't get hung up on whether or not the statement is "right." What good is an exchange like this going to do you?

Prospect: You know what? We already have widgets that work just fine.

You: No, wait, these are better, it's a brand new model. Just listen.

What kind of message is the prospect getting from you?

Really, aren't you just saying something like this:

Prospect: You know what? We already have widgets that work just fine.

You: What are you interrupting me for? This is an entirely different type of product, you fool; it's even better than what you've got now.
   Now be quiet and let me finish.

Don't do it.

Don't send those kinds of signals. They lose sales. Instead, repeat the prospect's objection, then reassure the prospect that you can overcome the obstacle in such a way that will make the prospect's business run more effectively or more profitably.

An example of exactly how to do this follows.

Step three: solving the problem

Of course, that's the third step, solving the problem that's been presented to you. That must be your focus, because that's the prospect's focus. Here's how it all might sound:

Prospect: You know what? We already have widgets that work just fine.

You: Oh, okay, so you have a widget service now?
Well, I'll tell you, Mr. Smith, that's something I've heard from a lot of people, including many of the clients we've been working with to improve their effectiveness in this area. Their feeling on it, eventually, was that our results really spoke for themselves.

There. Isn't that a more relaxed, professional approach?

Wouldn't you feel justified in continuing a conversation with someone who said that to you, whether or not you had widgets? Wouldn't it seem worth your while to at least hear what the person had to say?

At this point, you'll probably be in a much better position to pick up where you left off. But don't be overhasty in doing so. If the problem has not been solved to the prospect's satisfaction, it's pointless to try to move on. Stay with your prospect, and work things out at his or her pace, not yours.

As you've probably noticed, the basic turnaround technique I've just outlined is similar to what we saw in the qualifying stage. It's just a matter of adapting it to the situation that's in front of you at the moment, and taking a little more time than you did when you were qualifying.

Identify the objection, preferably in such a way that you understand which of the six main categories it falls into; acknowledge the validity of the objection by repeating it to the client; do your darnedest to solve the problem that's been put in front of you by the prospect—and remember to use the basic turnaround technique.

That's how it all works.

The motives behind the objections

Here is a brief summary of the main objectives that typically underlie the six main kinds of objections, as well as some additional strategies for turning them around.

I'd recommend committing these six outlines to memory.

The Stall

The Motive: In this variation, the person is putting a roadblock in front of you—keeping the decision-making process from going forward. That doesn't necessarily mean that they've formed any strong feelings one way or the other about your product or service, but it does mean that they've decided to try to put things on hold for a while. Usually, this is so they can determine what it is that they really want to do—without being pressured.

The Strategy: Early on, it won't hurt anyone to let the prospect postpone a decision for a while; all you want is to be sure that you're not going to sit "on hold" forever. So your goal here is to set a specific timetable for future action.

Prospect: I would really have to talk to the manager first, and unfortunately, she's out for the rest of the afternoon.

You: Sure, I can understand that. I'll tell you what. Why don't I come back Tuesday and meet with you and your manager so we can talk about how we can help you out in this area? Is three all right?

Prospect: Maybe you could just send me something in writing.

You: No problem. I'll tell you what; why don't you give me the specs right now, and I'll make sure we get you a quote by mid-day tomorrow. I'll bring it by myself.

Prospect: We've got a really big project going; this week is really terrible. For now I'm just going to have to say it really doesn't look good.

You: Listen, I understand. I'll tell you what, why don't I come by next week when things aren't so rushed. How's next Tuesday at 3:00?

In each of the instances above, you'll get either a "green light" (an invitation to continue the process) or a "red light" (further stiffarming that will probably indicate the prospect really isn't interested).

The hidden objection

The Motive: Who knows?

Often, you will have absolutely no idea why the person to whom you're speaking objects to what you're saying, but you'll be quite certain that something is wrong somewhere. We call such situations hidden objections. They're usually quite difficult to address effectively.

The Strategy: As with the other kinds of objections, the basic principles of identify, validate, and solve still apply. One effective approach is to ask, "Have I done something wrong?" The prospect will probably be eager to avoid an awkward moment, reassure you that the problem is not your fault, and then give you more information, allowing you to fine-tune your approach. Here's how some other techniques might work in practice; what the prospect ISN'T saying is placed in parentheses.

Prospect: We're getting that for a very low price right now. (We haven't gotten that yet, but I'm afraid it will cost too much.)

You: Okay. Well, I can certainly understand being concerned with making the budget work. Listen, was there a specific figure you had in mind?

I'll tell you the reason I ask. Often we can work out a different kind of package for you at some very attractive rates.

Prospect: We're committed to this vendor. (You could be anybody, and I'm not handing over my business to any fool who walks in off the street.)

You: Oh, so you already have a widget service. You know, one of the things we've been able to do for some of the people in your industry is successfully complement an existing widget relationship. We've gotten some terrific recommendations on that score from XYZ Company and DEF Group; maybe you'd like to take a look at those.

Prospect: The president is happy with the status quo, and he doesn't want to see anything else. (I haven't mentioned this to anyone else at all—I just want to be sure not to rock the boat.)

You: All right, so it's something for the president to take a look at. Well, you know what we might do—we could work out a pilot program for a very low price. That would allow the president to see how well the program would work, and the risk would be minimal.

Note that all of the responses I've suggested avoid painting the prospect into a corner. They allow him or her some "breathing room" by not focusing on whether or not the facts as stated by the prospect are "true." Again, the only relevant "truth" is the prospect's.

The hard objection

The Motive: The third-most-common roadblock, the hard objection, actually makes one part of your job—the identification stage—quite simple. The prospect simply comes out and says what the problem is, and it's a doozy.

For example, you have an appointment with an individual who tells you that he is working with your competition, that he feels they deliver superior results, and that he has determined that their prices are significantly below yours.

Then he leans back in his chair and smiles briefly, as if to say, "Your move."

The Strategy: At this point, there's a pretty fair chance this individual is not going to end up doing business with you. That doesn't necessarily mean that you pick up your marbles and go home, but it does mean that you keep a certain amount of perspective. Remember the nineteen "no's"?

If you feel it's warranted, and if you can do so without polarizing the exchange, you should probably give the prospect your best shot.

Attempt to find an opening that will allow you to negotiate with your prospect; try setting a specific timetable that will allow you to cooperate with the prospect in setting up a relationship.

Take the heat off. Try to make the issue what the next step should be, rather than what the decision is. If you ask for a decision after this kind of objection, you're asking to hear "no." You get enough of that already.

Of course, one of the most frustrating situations any salesperson can face is the one in which the prospect informs you that the fundamental purpose of your visit—a belief that the product or service is of possible application—simply doesn't exist.

Theoretically, this sort of problem should have been

ironed out during the qualifying stage, but real life has a way of refusing to follow theoretical guidelines. Every once in a while, you're going to sit down in front of someone who says, "We don't think it's worth it. We have no faith in this kind of product. We simply don't think there's any use for it, and we've decided against it for the foreseeable future."

What do you do?

Start out by not setting your hopes too high. Then, keep your chin up. After all, what have you got to lose?

Prospect: We don't believe in widgets here.

You: Well, I can certainly understand that feeling, and I'll tell you why: a lot of the same clients I'm working with right now felt the exact same way. We've really been able to turn things around at XYZ Corporation, for instance, and they'd been in business for 64 years without using widgets.

Let me tell you a little bit about that program . . .

Prospect: Look, let me be honest with you. We tried this with your company in 1984 and it was a disaster. Why should it be any different this time?

You: Because we've changed. And I'll tell you what else: there are dozens of our clients who know we've changed and have come back to work with us again.

Mr. Prospect, I'm not going to try to pull

a fast one here—our company went through a very tough period a few years back, and we lost sight of the most important aspect of our business: customers.

We made some important changes both in our personnel and in the way we do business, and, let me tell you, we've won back most of the people who left us. I'll be honest, a lot of them swore they'd never talk to us again. XYZ Company felt much the same way as you do when I first spoke with them earlier this year. Now they're one of our best customers.

Let me do this: I'd like to work up a quote for you on this job. Compare it with anyone else's in the industry who can deliver our quality. I think you'll like what you see.

Can I come by next Tuesday and drop it off for you?

Prospect: We've got an in-house person who does that. It's working out quite well. Now, if you don't mind, I'm very busy, and frankly, I don't think there's much point in us discussing this any further.

You: Well, I can understand that, Mr. Prospect; because the issue is increasing your company's productivity, though, I think it may be relevant to look at the work we've done with some of the people in your field. Here's what I'd suggest. Let me arrange for a conference call with my contact at JJJ Company, Ann Brighton; she had an in-house program

---

that sounds similar to yours, and she's now very enthusiastic about what we're doing for her company. I'm certain you'll be interested in what she has to say. Can we call you? How does next Tuesday at 9:30 a.m. sound?

Remember, this is one of the most sensitive parts of any presentation, and the point at which the odds are heaviest against you. There is nothing to be gained by confronting or challenging the prospect; there is everything to be gained by trying to find points of cooperation. Without the prospect's cooperation, the entire exercise is meaningless.

The easy one

The Motive: This kind of objection is, as the name would suggest, relatively simple to overcome; yet it trips up far too many salespeople. Here's the scenario: the prospect puts up a roadblock, that, technically speaking, is an objection. However, to any reasonably adroit salesperson, it's quite clear that the person is in fact begging you for a reason to say "yes". This kind of objection practically turns around itself.

The Strategy: The best advice here is to be prepared. Often, in my seminars, I'll find that salespeople, ready for the killer objections, are most easily disoriented by the objections that should really give no one any trouble. Don't get taken by surprise!

Prospect: Look, I'm sorry, I'd need to have some kind of trial period. We don't go with anything that we can't be assured will work for us.

You: Well, if you're looking for a trial period, Mr. Prospect, I think I may have some good news for you. All our widgets are unconditionally guaranteed. You have ninety days to try them out; if you're not satisfied, we'll refund your money.

Prospect: This isn't going to work; for one thing, we need a guaranteed delivery date.

You: You know, Mr. Prospect, guaranteeing prompt setup is one of the areas we pride ourselves on. We can use an overnight service if necessary. You will get the widgets on time; you have my word on that.

Prospect: Our cash is too tight this month.

You: I can certainly understand that; believe me, I know it can be tough running a seasonal business! Here's what a lot of our clients do: they set up the program now, and we don't invoice for 45 days. I'd have to arrange it with my credit department, but I honestly don't think we'd have a problem with it.

After employing these techniques to deal with the easier objections, I'd suggest using a very powerful sales tool we learned about in the last chapter on closing: silence. Identify the problem, validate it, solve it, then BE QUIET. You'd be surprised how often the prospect will say, "Well, then, let's get started!"

One word of caution: don't make promises you can't keep. As we've seen, much of successful selling depends on having a base of satisfied clients. If you promise everyone you talk to that they'll have widgets in two weeks, and you routinely deliver in three months, word will get around.

The request for reassurance

The Motive: This occurs when the prospect has some doubts about the credibility of the product or service you're offering.

If you've done your work correctly, and have a top notch product or service to offer, this objection is usually quite simple to overcome.

The Strategy: What he or she wants is for you to give some solid examples of how your service has helped others, and could be expected to perform in the current setting.

Obviously, you should try to frame your examples in terms that have a direct application to the prospect's business.

Prospect: But our company is so large.

You: It sure is. That's one of the reasons I'm excited about this program. You know, XYZ company is pretty big, too—and they found that the system really benefited them.

Prospect: We only work with established firms.

You: Well, Mr. Prospect, I'm not going to tell

you we've been around as long as your company has, but we have been in business since 1984. And, you know, over that time, we've at least doubled in size every single year. Part of that is because of the success we've had working with companies like yours, such as. . .

Prospect: But our sales force is very young.

You: And that's exciting. That's a great environment to work in. You know, BBB company also has a very young sales force like yours, and the program worked especially well for them.

As you know by now, the discreet use of the names of satisfied clients in your presentation can make a big difference in any setting. When confronting a request for reassurance, it's just about mandatory.

Doubt and fear

The Motive: Did you ever decide to make a major purchase—a car, say, or an expensive gift for someone—and then, at the moment of truth, suddenly freeze up?

It happens to just about everyone at one time or another. For my part, I tend to hyperventilate uncontrollably around the first of the month when it's time to sign checks.

Seriously, though, a last-minute case of the jitters on your prospect's part is quite normal, and may actually be a positive sign.

The Strategy: As you might expect, the foundation of the turnaround technique remains the same, with the accent on a calm, confident approach to the problems the prospect is confronting.

Prospect: Gee, the market has been so volatile lately.

You: You know, I'll tell you something; many of my clients expressed that same fear, but they've actually done quite well with their investments.

Prospect: I don't know. A car is really a big deal. I mean, you don't buy one every day.

You: Yep. That's true. A car sure is a major purchase for most of us. But it seems to me as if you're really ready for this one.

Prospect: What if it doesn't work?

You: Can I tell you something? I've talked with a lot of people about these seminars, and most of them do tend to get a little case of the butterflies when faced with a project like this. After all, it's a new approach! But the important thing to keep in mind is that we guarantee our program works when used properly.

"The bum in the bank" . . . or: the many dangers of judging your prospect ahead of time

Many of the "objections" salespeople say they encounter are theirs, not the prospect's.

Don't judge the prospect ahead of time. Give him or her a fair shot.

If, for some reason, you have doubts about where the prospect stands, for goodness sake, don't ask questions endlessly, with no real purpose. Once you start to prejudge a contact, or give them the third degree with overaggressive "probing" techniques, you're probably not too far from quickly deciding, based on their "wrong" answers, that you can't be bothered with seeing them.

More often than you think, you will have made a very big mistake.

We once did a program for a certain bank in New York City. After the seminar, one of the managers pulled me aside, pointed discreetly, and said, "See that guy over there?"

I looked over toward the shabbiest, dirtiest, most unkempt man I'd ever seen inside a bank. "What about him?" I asked.

"That man," the manager explained, "has just over one million dollars deposited in this bank."

Now, I thought the manager had wanted my help in escorting this "vagrant" off the premises! Shows you what you get for thinking.

It doesn't matter what you think of the prospect. It only matters what the prospect thinks of you—your product or service, your presentation, your attitude. Don't make the prospect meet some imaginary set of standards you've set up, some yardstick you use to measure a "good sale." A sale is a sale. Let the prospect write the rules.

Further insights on the neglected art of handling objections

Many salespeople don't want to spend fifteen hours figuring out how to turn around an objection—they want to get to the meat, fast. With them in mind, I've condensed some additional key points on this important subject into a few paragraphs (below). You may want to refer to these summaries a little later for easy reference.

Ready?

When your prospect tries to stall, the best approach is usually to offer a specific timetable for further action on the matter. (This will not only leave you with a clear view of your next step, but also help to smoke out those who are simply too wishy-washy to tell you they aren't seriously interested.)

When the objection is that the product or service costs too much, you usually have several options. You can discuss the advantages of a lower-priced version (as we did above in recommending the A-43). You can pro-rate the costs to place the issue in the proper perspective (point out that the A-43 will end up costing only a few cents a day over the course of a year). You can compare your price to that of a competitor or to the "cost" of continuing to do business without the product or service.

You may get an "objection" that's vague or unclear, leaving you with no idea of how to proceed. In these cases, it's generally best to come out and ask the client where the problem is.

Some objections are tougher than others. It will be very difficult indeed to turn around an objection like this:

Prospect: Guess what? I just bought one of your competitor's units last week, the Cheap'n'Dirty, Inc. Hyperfraxilator. I got it for nothing; my brother works for Cheap'n'Dirty.

On the other hand, many objections will be much easier to address, particularly if the prospect is reminded how "other people used to say exactly the same thing."

Prospect: We like the color green here at our company, and all the fraxilators I've ever heard about have been red.

You: Actually, that's no problem, sir. Many of our customers prefer green fraxilators—that's why we've come out with eleven different shades of green on the A-43.

Remember that objections are part of the sales cycle. There's no personal dig at you if the prospect's father-in-law is employed by one of your rival companies. Such a situation is one of the many, many objections you'll encounter over the course of a business day. Some of them you'll be able to turn around; some you won't.

SUMMARY
Chapter Eight:
Objections

✔ Context is crucial in interpreting your prospect's objection.

✔ Every objection can be broken down into one of six basic types: Stall, Hidden, Reassurance, Doubt, Hard, and Easy.

✔ In addressing a prospect's objection, the first step is to identify it.

✔ The second step is to validate it.

✔ The third step is to solve it.

✔ Even in the more advanced stages, one basic turn-around technique that is quite effective is a variation on the "other people said the same thing" approach discussed in the chapter on qualifying. A great many successful applications of this technique are likely to be useful to you.

✔ Review thoroughly the various strategies for over-coming each of the six main objection groups.

✔ Don't judge the prospect ahead of time. Many "objections" salespeople say they encounter are theirs, not the prospect's.

Chapter Nine

The New Sales Economy

**My vacation, or, how I went to Mexico and gained a
new perspective on the American marketplace**

I wouldn't call it an epiphany, really. Just one of those
flashes of insight you wish would come along more often. It
was the morning of the last day of my Mexican vacation; I
was in a large bazaar in Cancun looking for souvenirs for my
office staff.

Entering the marketplace, which was already bus-
tling with tourists and filled with the cries of vendors
hawking their wares, I wandered over to the first stall and
did a quick review of the merchandise. I noted without surprise that sombreros and clay pots dominated the table; after checking the prices, I strolled to the next stall to see
whether a better deal might be had elsewhere.

Hours passed under the hot Mexican sun as I ambled
from stall to stall, always browsing and never buying. At
last, hot and tired, I stopped at the stall positioned nearest
the exit of the fifty or so I had visited and made my purchases. No surprises, really: I selected an assortment of clay
pots and sombreros.

The wares were essentially the same from one stall
the the next. So were the prices. There was no real difference between the fellow I bought from and all the others I
had visited. It just so happened that at that moment, I was
ready to buy, and his was the stall closest to the exit.

Then came the dollar question. How do all those sellers survive selling essentially the same goods at essentially the same prices? I turned this issue over in my mind as I headed back to the hotel with my purchases. The answer I came up with was brutal in its simplicity: They survive because there are enough tourists to go around. The tourists come; they browse; they buy. If for some reason the tourists vanish from the scene, everyone's out of business.

In a way, this example is useful in analyzing selling in the United States, too. We Americans like to think of ourselves as a fiercely competitive nation, and of course, that's true—to a degree. Often, however, it seems to me that we let our emphasis on our competitive nature blind us to some of the larger truths of our selling environment. Specifically, I think we overlook the fact that our economy is *primarily market-driven*. Sure, there are breakthroughs and shakeouts and all the rest of those things, but the defining reality in my view is that of the *size and disposition of the marketplace* in this country.

Think about it for a moment. When a major new product or service comes along, the most important dynamic is not who has it, but *how people react to it*. Who has it and at what terms are important, but not *as* important as the movement of the marketplace. If you don't believe me, go out to your nearest electronics outlet and ask to buy a new eight-track tape player, a Betamax video system, or a Commodore home computer system.

IMPs, EMPs—and everybody else

As I have often said, sales fall into three categories. Given a minimal level of professionalism and product knowledge on your part, one group of prospects is pretty much going to go your way no matter what you do. Another group will get past all the early stages, but will go to someone else—or not buy at all—despite your best efforts. The third group consists of prospects who could go either way. It is by securing that final group that the superior salespeople set themselves apart from the pack.

That third group is the group that calls for something extra. That third group calls for real selling skills. That third group is the group this book is designed to help you deal with.

If you've gotten this far in the book, you've realized by now that the emphasis in my system is always on selling to *people*, and not to the institutions those people represent. Still, it is instructive for our purposes to take a moment now to classify the types of companies you are likely to deal with.

The way I see it, there are three kinds of companies in the American economy: those already in your marketplace (I'll call them IMPs); those entering your marketplace (EMPs); and those well outside your marketplace (I call them "cloistered buyers"). Let's look at each category in turn.

IMPs are in the market to buy. My company became an IMP recently when I decided to get a new copier for the office. No one had to convince me I needed a copier; I already knew that. The only question was which one I would ultimately buy. As an IMP, I had certain other key characteristics, as well.

IMP companies . . .

❏ *Are looking for solutions.* They have identified a problem, need, or desire and are looking for a way to get that requirement met.

❏ *Are ready to buy.* A decision to buy has been made within the company.

❑ *Are likely to be knowledgeable.* They have probably either researched the topic or bought the product or service before from you or someone else. This means you will have to be highly creative to match the price and quality levels they have already become familiar with.

❑ *Have a strong sense of what they want to buy.* They see the salesperson essentially as an order taker and tend to feel that they should be able to dictate the terms of the sale.

❑ *May want to better their existing deal.* They may be trying to "trade up" by moving to another vendor or may be trying to improve payment terms, price, or some other component of the current agreement. They may simply want something new; they may want to deal with more than one vendor on principle because they wish to keep people "on their toes."

So IMPs have already made the decision to buy. What about EMPs, those entering the marketplace? Well, EMPs *could* buy. They think they have a need; they may even have come to some conclusions internally. But no decision has been made yet. If you, the salesperson, can get to that company *before* it enters the marketplace, you'll stand a better chance.

What else can be said about EMPs?

EMP companies . . .

❏ *Have a need, want, or desire for which they think they know the solution.* No decision has been made yet, however.

❏ *Have only recently determined the possibility of a need for your product or service.* (This usually means that they have not done much research or spoken with your competition yet.)

❏ *Have not yet taken the direct step of contacting a vendor, but are likely to call someone in the future, thereby becoming IMPs.*

❏ *Probably need something completely new to them.* EMPs are likely to be starting from scratch.

Now let's turn to cloistered buyers or companies. Remember, they can be a Fortune 500 firm or a small outfit, or even a division within a company. The main point is, these people are happy doing what they're doing. They don't really need you—at any rate, this is what they would say if asked. In any event, they're satisfied with things the way they are.

Cloistered buyers or companies

❏ *Have something that works for them, something that is not necessarily what you do.*

❑ *May be unaware that you exist.*

❑ *May be surrounded by business "buffers" such as accountants, CPAs, the controller, the owner, the family, or company history.*

❑ *Have no need to buy.* (That is to say, they have not reached any conclusion that leads them to believe they have a need for your product or service.)

Sound impossible? Well, it isn't. Challenging, yes. Impossible, hardly. In fact, my experience tells me that if you approach a certain number of cloistered buyers several years in a row, sooner or later you'll win over the majority of these contacts by sheer persistence.

You'll gain, by my estimates, about 15 percent of these sales in the first year; another 15 percent in the second, which, combined with your sales in the first year, will bring you up to 30 percent; and another fifteen percent in the third year, bringing the total to 45 percent. If you keep the process up for five years, you will have converted roughly 75 percent of those seemingly impossible sales. Even if you do lose some of these sales to attrition and the natural decline of your prospect base, you can still expect to convert well over half of these tough prospects over a period of five years.

So what's your strategy?

I'm not saying you should drop the IMP and EMP companies and concentrate on those outside the marketplace. I don't advocate neglecting any market for your service. The key is prioritizing. Develop different approaches or strategies for selling to each of the three categories.

Let's consider companies already in the marketplace, companies that are ready to buy. To sell these companies, you have to keep visible. That's crucial. You'll need to make calls constantly, send innumerable reminders, and perhaps invest in advertising, public relations work, or trade shows. You'll need to introduce new products. With IMPs. it really is "out of sight, out of mind"—and out of a sale.

EMPs, those companies just entering the marketplace, are a somewhat harder sell. Visibility is important here, too, but it isn't enough. To succeed with EMPs, you'll need to distinguish yourself from the crowd. A generic, white-bread presentation won't make it with this group. Your pitch will need to emphasize reassurance, examples, and plenty of compelling stories and parables that show how you can help these people. Education about the advantages your product or service carries over the competition is the order of the day.

As for the cloistered buyers, the emphasis there, naturally, is on breaking into a closed market. Here are some of the steps you'll need to take:

To reach cloistered buyers . . .
- ❏ Prospect.
- ❏ Target specific industries.
- ❏ Develop leads aggressively.
- ❏ Uncover sources via referrals.
- ❏ Identify the decision maker early on in the process.
- ❏ Introduce your product or service and company.
- ❏ Present.
- ❏ Use solid examples.
- ❏ Educate for the long term.

❏ Accept that you will often have to pass
for now and come back.

Buck the trend

Most American companies go to the IMP companies
to sell. These sales are need-driven. They're not driven by
the salesperson. A smaller but still substantial number go
after the EMPs. A harder sell, but not a big stretch.

There is a big chunk of the market that is shunned:
the cloistered buyers. And why? Because most of our sales
representatives have no real training in how to go after
them.

Remember the Mexican bazaar. You are playing a
market-oriented game. By reaching out to the cloistered companies, you will, in effect, be placing your stall at the highest traffic point in the bazaar. That means you'll get
exposure to a lot more potential customers. So the other
vendors think some of them are too tough to sell. That's
their problem. Commit to reaching that market anyway.
That's where the growth potential is.

And I'm talking about long-term growth potential.
Once you penetrate that part of the market, the relationships you establish will be more enduring. Granted, success won't be automatic. To succeed with cloistered
buyers, you must become their partners in growth. You'll
need to sharpen your sales skills as well as your creativity,
coming up with creative price solutions and other tailor-
made responses. In other words, you must learn to see
yourself as much more than an order taker. You're inven-
tive. You care about your clients' needs. You're there to
help. You have knowledge, skills, and solutions. And
you're a partner in something new.

Buck the trend. The rewards are waiting for you.

SUMMARY
Chapter Nine:
The New Sales Economy

✔ The defining reality of our economy is the size and disposition of the marketplace.

✔ There are three main kinds of buyers: IMPs, EMPs, and cloistered buyers.

✔ Cloistered buyers represent an avenue of real opportunity for today's salespeople.

Chapter Ten

Summing Up

On your own . . ?
Now comes the tough part.

Putting any set of precepts and ideas into action can be difficult. Starting from ground zero with your sales work, and perhaps beginning to undo some old habits that may be standing in the way of your success, isn't going to happen overnight.

In my experience, though, it takes 21 days.

You may be familiar with the theory that, if you want to get rid of an old habit or permanently establish a new way of doing things, the best course of action is to promise yourself to give the new idea a fair shot for three calendar weeks. By that point, the theory goes, you'll have become rehabituated, and you can depend on the new, more positive routines you've set for yourself.

You know what? It works.

Don't ask too much of yourself, though. If there's one major area in your work you'd particularly like to improve—your prospecting skills, say—sit down with your calendar, give yourself a target date, and then work like the dickens to incorporate the principles relating to that topic for the next three weeks.

Then proceed throughout *your* list of areas in which you'd like to see improvement. Keep the same 21-day format. My bet is, you'll see results.

One of the points I like to make in my seminars is that every salesperson should be willing to take on the role of his or her own personal sales manager. What that means is, you take responsibility for your performance. You review your progress. You assess your performance. Approaching your sales work in this way—almost as though you're reporting to yourself every morning—can make the "on-your-own" aspects of sales work more workable

A final word

As a salesperson, you're probably a little less tied to the clock than most workers. However, as you may have picked up by now, I believe your time is extremely valuable. Don't fall into the trap of doing mediocre work during supposed "slow periods." Give it all you've got now, today, this minute. It's all you have.

Where I work, we have a little variation on the "have a nice day" greeting people use so often. To tell you the truth, we've sort of banished "have a nice day" from our company vocabulary. Not because we're mean-spirited, but because we like to remind ourselves of how important it is to seize the opportunities that present themselves on any given business day.

We remind each other to "make it a productive day." And more often than not, that's just what we do. It's with that ever-pertinent reminder that I leave you, because your success, like ours, is completely up to you. Make the most of today.

Make it a productive day!

Index

About the Author

Stephan Schiffman has trained over 250,000 salespeople at firms such as Airborne Express, AT&T Information Systems, Chemical Bank, Manufacturers Hanover Trust, Motorola, Prudential-Bache, Smith Barney, and U.S. Healthcare. Mr. Schiffman, president of DEI Management Group, is the author of *Cold Calling Techniques (That Really Work!)*, *The 25 Sales Habits of Highly Successful Salespeople*, *The 25 Most Common Sales Mistakes (and How to Avoid Them)*, and *Stephan Schiffman's Telemarketing*. He lives in the New York City area.